THE GROUND OF OUR BEING

Reflections on farming, life, and other challenging pursuits

Paul A. Myers

High Peregrine Press
679 Henry Road, Gibsons, BC, V0N 1V2
highperegrinepress@gmailcom

Printed in Canada
Second Printing, 2018

ISBN printed version 978-1-9995038-0-2
ISBN digital version 978-1-9995038-1-9

For Violet, Leo, Luca, and Sawyer
And for their good tomorrow

Introduction

Look on the horizon. It is just there. Do you see it? True, it seems to disappear into the mist sometimes. But other times it feels as though you could almost touch it. A vision is like that: one moment elusive, another moment unmistakable. Of course there are days, hard days and dark days, when I doubt that I ever saw it. But then I remind myself that others have seen it too, so how can it be a mirage? We are those who share a vision for the day when swords will be beaten into ploughs, and spears into pruning hooks. Who live as travellers through transitional times, who long for that better future, and that better place. We see a land that is blessed and that blesses, and a community living in peace. Where there is enough for all, and where every person knows their neighbour.

But in order for a vision to 'become', it needs more than merely belief in it. So we work, and all the while as workers we are learners, apprentices of life and of the land. Said St. Augustine, 'solvitur ambulando'. It is solved by walking. The questions of how to live by and for a vision are resolved when we just begin to step forward. Feet on the ground. It's that simple: in the everyday doing of the work that grows slowly but inexorably, we learn. We start small. We start now.

Dawn and I live on eight acres of land. For millennia the site was inhabited by the First Peoples, where they harvested food and game in the great forest that grew here. Just over a century ago the kings of timber arrived, and the forest fell: massive Red Cedar and Douglas fir. With the great trees gone, the land covered itself in scrub growth, alder, and then hemlock again. On this site a traditional farm emerged. They called the farm 'Brookbank', perhaps after Chaster Creek that dances along its border, or perhaps merely for the magical cadence in the name. In its heyday Brookbank was a complete homestead farm, with orchards, commercial food crops and hay, livestock, and draft horses for the heavy labour. Brookbank began to decline about the time most small farms did in our country, until eventually all farm activity virtually ceased. With our arrival, Brookbank entered a new phase. By recapturing the wisdom of the past, and by applying regenerative farm practices today, this land reawakens as a farm and more.

So much more, because this land has found its way into me, right straight into my heart. How can it not? Like the good mother, it provides food for me, and like the good teacher, lessons. So I walk into the future with my admittedly lofty vision of change, and yet begin again in my latest kindergarten of life. The experience is full, there is work, and it is joyous to me. As you read the pages that follow you may want to go slowly, perhaps one entry a week, making your journey of thought align with the journey of a full-season farm year. My hope is that you will be encouraged to see something hopeful in your own today, and yes, off on that horizon, in your tomorrow also.

My Dirty Old Man

My father grew up poor in south side Chicago, a clapboard house with no insulation, and rail tracks out back where the freight trains rolled past on their way to the Blue Island Yards. Like many, his family appropriated a small plot off the siding there to eke out some vegetables, and to keep a few hens. Today we might call it something like "urban guerrilla gardening," but in the meagre 1930's it was perfectly normal behaviour. Everyone did it, or at least, everyone poor did. As a child my Dad worked that rank, oily soil, and though he hated chores, the soil did what soil does: it went into his skin.

Then came Abundant America. Giddy with victory, flush with resources, beguiled by prosperity. And the concrete trucks came and made freeways, and suburbia was born. The pull of 'more, better, and bigger' became inexorable. Food gardens gave way to more lawns, fringed by a regimented brew of ornamental foliage, incongruous and—save for eye appeal alone—without function. Pampas Grass beside Ajuga beside Viburnum beside Jade Plant beside Mock Orange. That's how I grew up, a kid on a Schwinn bike riding over fresh blacktop, past yards festooned in green bling.

My Dad bought in to the prevailing doctrine of the times. But, just like all of us, he never really sloughed his roots altogether. Or rather, the dirt never really got out of him. So we had lawns, but we also had vegetables. As a child, I did chores in that garden. And, as I would later discover, the soil did what it does. When my father died last year at age ninety-three, his body was completely expended. But all around his home, lawns long since only a memory, he had vegetables growing.

My partner Dawn's story is similar: a love for a garden that came from her father. This is the story of nearly all of us, in fact, because this is how life once was, not so long ago. When our mothers and fathers (city folk, country folk, no matter) got their nails messy, grew a bit of food. When they saw seedlings grow, blossom, and fruit. When they harvested and served. They experienced this everyday joy, and had a measure of food sovereignty too. We don't need to reach back far to find a farmer/gardener in everyone's lineage. It was not so long ago. Perhaps, then, it is not so far from returning. Look closely at your hands. I'm venturing you will see it, just beneath your skin.

What a Dreamer, They Say

Some years ago I read Chris Hedges' work "Empire of Illusion," a book forecasting economic, political, environmental, and moral collapse. It was brilliant, it was riveting, and it was totally depressing. My already refined cynicism and my angst for the future were fed a ghoulish feast of the damned.

But I have since changed my intellectual diet, and I am not likely to read such a book any time soon. This is not because I disagree with Hedges, for I rarely do. It is also not because I have closed my eyes to the realities of the shadow sides of life. I have not. My reasons are more intentional, and more personal, than that. It is because I have lately discovered that cynicism and angst never achieved anything good in me. It is because that while the world of peak oil, profiteers and politicians lingers, I know now that theirs is not the only world, and that if change for the better is not achieved in a year or a decade, it will be achieved nevertheless. And it is because I am purposing at last to embrace my finitude, and to resist the ignorant fetish that I must fix everything until it is perfect. After all, the goal is not perfection, but transformation, both personal and social. Are these easy lessons for me? Hell no. Have I learned them well? Not yet. But I have sampled their sweetness, and now like young Edmund in C.S. Lewis' *Narnia* stories and his craving for Turkish Delight, I just want more.

I credit this new journey of thought to several compelling teachers, but none are as significant as the simple existence of life on the land. Here at Brookbank Farm my home, I am surrounded by the rhythmic, inexorable actions of Nature: a seed sprouting, a tree flowering, a tadpole in a pond. It's a veritable pageant, in fact, a grand show-by-doing of the unstoppable abundance to occur.

Of course, I still wake up grouchy sometimes, I do. I still catch myself in moribund fascination with the evening news. But the seed is there now, and it will grow. It is inevitable. Just as sure as spring cannot be cancelled, so goodness and plenitude will finally prevail.

The Blessed Mess

I hate a mess. I hate a mess more than I hate cucumbers (for which I am locally famous). But at least I come by my penchant for tidiness honestly. There is heredity. My father, a mariner who always kept everything 'ship shape', married my mother, a world class clean-aholic. Together they made me. There is education. My graduate schooling included three spins through the exactitude of Protestant theology. There is environment. Among other important lessons, I was reared to understand that one should not sit in mud when a chair is available.

You can imagine therefore that the realm of Nature and I regularly come to loggerheads. And never more than in springtime. I want neatness. She wants the grass to grow a foot in a week. I want containment. She wants the dandelions to go viral. I want straight rows and clean borders and uniform plantings. She is boundless, a dervish of fecundity, reaching far, a hormonal teenager, an anti-establishment, post-Christian, pre, post and expost-Modern in-the-now of this explosive reproductive moment prophetess. "Diversity!" she cries uncouthly. "Abundance!" her placard indecently reads. "Free love for all plants, animals, birds, fish, insects, reptiles, spiders, microorganisms and anything else with any spark of life!" She flings arms outward and the endless concoction of seeds fly higgledy-piggledy to the far reaches of Creation. How did it come to this? That I should exalt appearances, while she lauds abundance? That I should (still! at my age!) be tempted to think Better Homes and Gardens, while she has only ever wanted this place to be a home?

But there is a mystery afoot, a dialectic at play. For in all that reckless one-time abandon for Life, she is anything but random, and anything but chaotic. When I shinny down from my pedestal of effrontery the view at ground level is much better. I see that there is both expansiveness and yet containment. There is eruption and yet systems. Far flung, and yet peaceful. On the one hand, Nature seems to have the most haphazard disregard of bounds. On the other, she is utterly calculated and lawful to herself, more than the sternest puritan ever was.

Nature is life, and Nature teaches life. It teaches us again that at the heart of truth lies paradox. As the seed that must die to live. As the sunrise that thrills us until the earthquake that buries us. As a breath, with it's at-once 'always' of oxygen and 'never' of carbon dioxide. As the order we crave, and the turmoil we live.

Surrounding Myself With You

As to imitating the perfect farmer (Nature) we're having ourselves an experiment. Here's the principle at play: because Nature is smart, resourceful, and optimistic to grow, she forms alliances between organisms. Yes, assuredly, there is a battle for soil, water, and light. But that's only one side of the story. In fact, for every skirmish there are a thousand truces. A tree provides dapple to a plant that would otherwise sizzle in full sun. The plant, in turn, offers nitrogen to the tree. A bee harvests pollen and nectar as food for its colony. In return, the flower, shrub, or tree is cross-pollinated. Without the synergy of two both would perish. And when we look closely, we see that such alliances are not limited to simple unions of two. Instead Nature has created a festival of interdependency, a Mardi Gras of cosmic scale, where the outcome is a colourful, boisterous Conga line of fun. Plants and trees are the foundation and they lead the way. But lining up behind are the isopods, spiders, birds, fish, mammals, and reptiles. Hands on the hips in front of you! It's a regular cross-taxonomic dance of touching and swaying. Of course, these shared alliances are more than about fun; they make for a productive, resilient, and beautiful world. The thriving garden of human making is one that mimics this principle of Nature: a diverse gathering of cooperative, reciprocating plants and other organisms.

In the parlance of permaculture farming, this symbiosis is sometimes called a "guild." With a food bearing or other tree as a foundation, a confraternity of beneficial plants within its environs is created. If you stroll around Brookbank you will see row crops, to be sure. But you also will see a madcap assortment of 'guilding' in process: lupine, kale, rhubarb, horseradish, yarrow, and willow coppices gathered around a Hazelnut tree; red clover, comfrey, chives, and garlic beneath an apple tree. Of course, the perfect plant guild for our climate, our very land, has yet to be written. Hence, we have our experiment. In time we'll know what works best.

Here again I must segue from soil to soul, for we have a slam dunk of metaphor. Why should we also not imitate Nature here? Forming human alliances of the right kind. Bringing around us those who benefit us (and we, them), who help us to be optimistic to grow, who touch and sway with us to the celebration of life as a journey of hope.

For years unnumbered (and for reasons I may never understand) I made my alliances with a host of social strays, political sceptics, urbane pessimists, burnt out war resistors, and in the otherwise thrilling game of life, fence sitters. Well, friends, no longer. I'm out to find the friendlies now. To spit and shake, and then to mutually prosper. I'm moving into that light now. To surround myself with those who inspire me, who carry neither bad nor fake but good news, and who defy me with unvarnished love to become all that my life will be: a productive, resilient, and beautiful life. If that's you I'm describing, c'mon over. I'm surrounding myself with you.

Do the Hokey Pokey

Those of you who have visited Brookbank Farm know that Dawn and I have been working steadily to reclaim and restore this site to become a regenerated farm that provides food for our community. To do so we try to work with Nature, mimicking her movements, and listening when she speaks. Of course, we also nudge the process along. For instance, after we studied for some time the patterns of water flow on the land we undertook a large project, building a series of three connecting ponds and waterways.

But it's not always easy to see Nature's movements or to hear her voice, and not least because a bend-of-knee attitude runs against my—okay, full disclosure here—control-freak, manipulate-the-outcomes, Calvinistic-domination-of-Earth machismo that was drilled into me in my formative years. Dawn, bless her, is much better than I am at adapting. Here I provide two examples. First, there is Canaan Field, which we opened for field crop production a few years back. For two seasons we grew some brassicas and kale there but despite the good soil, without smashing success. We know now that it just happens to be one of those spots on the land where the undulations of blue clay beneath the topsoil rise a little too high, making for consistently high ground water. We could perhaps plant bog blueberries there. But when Dawn saw a host of new pioneer alders sprouting there she heard Nature. "Let it reforest here." So that is just what we are doing.

The second example is one of simple wonder. Our Toulouse geese got themselves hot and bothered. Eggs a poppin', we ate fine omelettes for a spell. Then one of the ladies decided to brood in a giant old cedar stump. She settled in, and as befits all mothers-to-be, promptly became violently protective of her (future) family. Hissing at us from forty feet away, we didn't go near. But a mama goose must incubate her eggs for thirty-five days, which is a long haul in a cedar stump. We might have plotted some scheme to steal the eggs, put them in an incubator, set the temperature and humidity just right, and turn them twice daily for a month. But again Dawn simply said, "Let's just see what happens." Well, what happened is displayed here: ten goslings, hale, whole, and cute as Heck.

It is vital that we learn to know when to exert ourselves for the outcomes we seek, and when not. When to put a foot in and when to put a foot out.

Counterpower

If I just had a little more....
    Time
    Money
    Education
    Freedom
    _____ (fill in your reasons here).

We spend years of our lives doing what we have to do, but not always what we want to do. Granted, there are certain necessities to be looked after. I'm not one for falling into scarcity and want. But how did it happen that those necessities became so many, so ubiquitous, and well, so necessary? Take, for instance, telecommunications and the Internet. Last night we revisited our monthly expense in that category. Despite all the adverts telling me what a great deal we are getting, it's stupidly expensive, far more than we ever used to spend.

It's no revelation that our society is driven by the engine of consumption. Every wander through the store, every radio spot, every secret comparison we make to others tells us that we lack. "If I just had a little more..." So it's off to work we go. We don't need to be happy. We need the highest paying job to meet the ever growing list of necessities.

Of course, we've been hoodwinked; we have. And here are my three very best reasons why: First, consumption is less like an engine and more like the Blob. Run. Scream, but if that's the strategy we will never get ahead of it. It will grow larger every time it eats another body. Second, 'new' is definitely pretty, definitely shiny. I get that. But 'new' is only new as long as it's new. Crap! Why didn't someone tell us? It's a one night stand! The first bit of tarnish will be there before breakfast! Finally, every moment spent 'working' in a work that is not our actual joy is a small death. Of our creativity. Of our calling in life. Of our world changing, nonviolent, counterpower against the lumbering, dying behemoth of old.

Now to the joy. As a complement to her love of farming, Dawn has lately found a new passion-as-work (or possibly it found her). She shows me her latest willow basket with the unfettered happiness that emanates from those who know they have made a beautiful something. Goodness, she's bouncing up and down over it. Her creativity, her aptitude, and her ingenuity are radiating like sunbeams. It's nice to be in that company. But we get this, right? *It's not work for her.*

If I just had a little more...
    Courage to follow my heart
    Indifference to the Blob
    Faith in the counterpower of creativity.

Who would think that a willow basket can do all that?

Who would think that the passion in us might change the economies of the world?

E Aye E Aye O!

Two former urbanites have lately learned why farmers traditionally get up early. Okay, I suppose everyone already knows the answer to that: to milk the cows, of course. What I mean to say is that two former urbanites have lately been experiencing animal patterns and needs, which begin well before we are feeling ready to meet them. So we take turns. Clad in a bathrobe carrying buckets of feed, we shuffle over dewy grass in our worn Crocs to release the geese and chickens from their safe havens, who greet the morning with much ballyhoo. Meantime the dogs are already bounding about their domains. Friends, the contrast is stark: their animation and spiritedness set against our drossy steps, looking like the crazies we are, and a dawning instinct to go make a stiff coffee.

We love it. We love that animals are so very sentient, with so much to teach us, and with a very rightful place on any farm that is what I call, 'full circle.' To watch little piggies rooting side by side, lined up and pushing like so many snow ploughs on a Quebec highway. To see the geese waddle past in single file with such orderliness, only to have riotous sex in the pond. To observe the dogs Mikayla and Bodie dig a hole with all the fury of title fighters. Why now? Why there? What do they seek? What is their lesson?

We care for them, and they in turn have purpose to us, and care for us. The farm animals provide food, turn soil, eat pests, and leave behind their most welcome soil amendment. And the mutts? They run off the odd deer or raven, and on behalf of their cohorts, they lick you in the face until you get out of bed.

Once we stayed out late amid city lights and the revelry they gleamed on. Once we rose lazily sometime before lunch. But we find a greater fullness now, and a deeper gratitude. Sure, at first light we look like Hell. So wince at the sight of us if you must, because after that there isn't much else about this scene not to like.

Defeating the Defeatist Within

The instinct is to be eternal. Plant, animal, bird, fish, microorganism, doesn't matter. Everything living wants to stay that way. When we swat a fly, it is, with its last mortal act as resistant as any other creature. Feint, dodge, fight or flee. Win or lose, it will try. Every day at Brookbank Farm, in some way or another, I see this struggle. This is simply the impulse of all life: to be alive.

It is, of course, ultimately a battle already lost. But I am thinking right now not so much about the end as the interim, about the sheer energy in all things living that pushes them past the present turmoil of being alive, the dangers, the depressions, the inexorable decline, and the "false endings." I am thinking about this energy because lately, and quite inexplicably, I have been feeling down. Such feelings inhabit me from time to time. There is no pinpointing some or another external reason for their mysterious visitations. "I lost my job!" "My family is in disarray!" "I'm broke again!" "My ball team sucks!" None of these. The feelings are neither timely nor untimely. Precipitated by who knows what, they simply come and go on their own schedule.

Because they just are, I am called from time to time to live with and through them until they are not. Sometimes I am counselled by others to not try to fix my emotions, or perhaps to 'surrender' and accept where I am. Hindu, Christian, Muslim, aetheist. All have some form of managing our unmanageables with quiet submission. *'En hypomene'* said Simone Weil. "I am waiting in patience." This is such wise counsel. Embracing our limitations, and our near powerlessness to arrange our feelings, is a worthy aspiration. I recommend it for all.

But then, as if the yang beside yin, there are those plants, animals, birds, fish and microorganisms offering a certain counter-counsel. They teach me the equal necessity of tapping the impulse within, of pushing through the hard parts with intention, and with the raw determination of being *alive*. For being alive, fully in the now and in the many false endings, is a very wondrous experience. In fact, why would we want it to be any other way? For here is where our creativity is born, where meanings emerge, where transcendence is met, where adventure occurs, and where we discover that we are stronger than we ever knew.

Do we let go, or do we take hold? Do we accept the grace or find the grit? The answer is, 'Yes, we do'.

Living In the Time Between

Has politics ever been more divided? Possibly, but the real question is, has it ever been more *tawdry*, reduced as it is to name calling, Tweets and counter-Tweets? These nationwide sideshows, these supersized schoolkids taunting one another ("Teacher, Teacher I declare, I see someone's underwear!"). It would all be so entertaining, if only it were just entertainment.

It isn't. It is real, and while it probably does not have all the importance we assign to it (because after all, politics has always been a capricious lover), politics and society with it does at least seem to be at a juncture. Which way will we go? It is as though we are standing in a hospital hallway: turn one direction and we are in Palliative Care. Turn the other and we are in the maternity ward. In this period of change surely both have a place. But the future, thank you, is where the smiles are. In Palliative Care a paradigm is dying, wizened now and yet not wiser, struggling against the inevitable, slipping into a state of defenceless and with it, spells of dementia. Apparently this dying is going out rather loudly too, Tweeting its resistance all the way. Meanwhile at Maternity the 'already but not yet' waits for the passage to be fully dilated. In the 1st century BCE ancient peoples used this very metaphor. '*Hodinin*' they said of waiting for the new age. "The birth pains."

If I could, I would credit my thoughts of this dying and birthing world to an interesting read, or to a compelling speaker on YouTube or Ted Talks. I'm sure there are plenty out there saying it better than me. Instead I credit the farm. You see, I keep getting struck by the 'otherness', perhaps by the 'nevertheless', of the farm experience. I see a pole bean, and against the earth sagging under the weight of flagpoles without number, that bean growing skyward seems to me like a more worthy standard bearer of our future. I see a plenteous blueberry bush, and against the message of scarcity and fear, it is quietly heralding a word of trust. I hear the chickens clucking and the pigs snorting, and against the din of a thousand parliamentary acts, they sound to me like the voices of midwives in a new world coming. The garden, the farm, is our dilated passage. We are in the hardest throes now of *Hodinin*. But we will be born.

DIY

Perfectionists of the world, I feel your pain. It must be very smooth, no blemishes. It must be unbroken, no Scotch tape. It must be tidy, no weeds. No flaws, no stains, no system errors. And that's just the baseline. For the advanced perfectionists there's more. We want it that way *the first time,* and we want it that way *every time*. To see anything less is agony, shafts of pain behind the eyes. Shuddering, we turn away, to cast our visionary gaze instead to a horizon all neatly covered in square paving stones.

We might blame our childhood home where even the pillow cases got ironed (they did), or those straights rows of tract homes we grew up in (they were), or our seventh grade P.E. instructor who wanted those push-ups done with military exactitude (he did). We might drop into a therapist's sofa and agonize over the dawning truth of a world of ambiguities (I have). But there's a cheaper and more expeditious way to get some balance back. Just do something of your own making, whether garden, project, or creative diversion. Do it yourself, and I guarantee that you will also get more circumspect about notions of flawlessness (and more to the point, notions of life) which no matter what some buffoon on TV or in your head is telling you, is never pressed flat, built straight, or done exact.

With time and double shots of reality I am getting better. I consider the seed propagation room I built here. It has a rain water catchment system, from roof to barrel to a secondary reservoir inside. From there a small pump provides a fine mist over the fifty-two flats that sit on movable racks. I'm rather proud of this creation, a MacGyver-style improvisation that, to my astonishment, is imperfect and yet works just fine. That I should be pleased with something somewhat flawed is a triumph in itself. But embracing the small deficiencies is not the real story here. The real story is that *I am proud* of the fact that I had to tear apart that rain water system three times before finally getting it right. Yes, you heard me. The first, second, and third attempts stunk and, pinch me, I am reveling in all that failure!

Let's try it, and try it with boldness. It will not be perfect, so let's go easy on ourselves as we learn. Give a little nod in respect to life's many imperfections. Self expression frees. In the workshop, in the garden, anywhere at all. If we try, by the very trying *and regardless of the final product*, we will thrive.

Unveilings

It could have been a scene out of *Avatar*. Mikayla trotting through the dense BC forest, and in her wake an effervescent wave of fairy dust. I gasped for the beauty of it, and then I squinted my aging eyes. Ah, not fairy dust, but something equally enchanted. My dog with her fulsome pantaloons and coquettish Toller hip sway was literally sweeping cottonwood seeds off the forest floor as she ran. *Whoosh*, and another wave like a bioluminescent tide would ripple slowly away. It was dreamlike. It was gorgeous. It took my breath away. When the path turned and opened into a clearing I saw cottonwood seeds everywhere, now flying past us. A blizzard in May.

We went home to an excited Dawn. "Come see all the tadpoles in Agapé pond! There are thousands of them!" So, I thought, she'd had her small epiphany today also. I was twice glad then, because there is nothing quite like a blast of childlike wonder when it comes in middle age.

A little visit like this from "on high" (or wherever it may come from) is a good thing. For long I have nurtured thoughts on all that is not right in our world and have reaped the feeling of dread for it. But now I was being rocketed away from these thoughts by a certain countervailing power. I took it in, content not to understand, but merely to revel.

Perhaps this is all I mean to say: let us be ready. Always ready to be momentarily carried away. To discover again the art of being keen to that 'aha' moment in our day, turning points that rebuke our pessimism, that awaken us to beauty, and that surprise us with joy. Perhaps that word of inspiration for this very day is whispered to us in the broccoli crowns forming, or tucked down inside the Nootka rose, or zooming by in the swallow's small beak. Something somewhere is just waiting to bring us delight.

Sui Generis

The first time I ever remember being distinctly embarrassed was in third grade class at Sonora Elementary School. My teacher was Mrs. Hansen, who favoured floral dresses and half eye glasses, and who I adored. We had been learning an eight-year old's Earth science, volcanic origins and such. Mrs. Hansen asked the question that doomed me. "Can anyone tell me how land was first formed?" Certainly she expected some response about those volcanoes again, pushing through primordial seas, or a word about 'continental drift', or even possibly ice ages carving valleys. At least with no rational answer, some respectful silence. Alas, I never owned a reputation for silence, respectful or otherwise. I eagerly put up my hand and when called on, said with scientific certitude: "There was great evil on the Earth and it was so bad that God caused rain to fall for forty days and forty nights, until there was water everywhere. Everybody died except for Noah and all the animals, who floated in an ark he had made. Then, after a while the storm on the outside became preferable to the stink on the inside so Noah sent birds out looking for dry land which eventually worked and that is how we got dry land."

It seemed a perfectly reasonable answer. After all, it came straight from the First Methodist Church. But after a few eternities of pin drop silence, somebody began to giggle, and then another, and then of course everybody caught it. Peals of undisciplined laughter erupted. Why, even Mrs. Hansen covered her mouth and did a little 'tee-hee'. I knew they were laughing at me, but I didn't know why. I do now. Attempting to turn a myth of religion into a scientific treatise is never smart, and often funny.

But here's the thing: I am getting old and childlike again, and there's a part to that ancient story that I feel good about revisiting. It's the *myth* of it. Myth as the veiled face of truth. Myth as a means for us to brush shoulders with the inexplicable, and to acknowledge that the cosmos is very deep, very puzzling, and utterly gorgeous. Laugh away, but I am a sucker for myth, fairly swept away by the mysteries all around me every day on this farm and in Nature everywhere. Such diversity. Such order. Such chaos. Power. Size. Visible. Invisible. Weight. Lightness. All of it. That a fava bean still does not sprout a magnolia. That an egret does not mate with a goose. That a golden plum hangs in waiting again, as it has for the last hundred years, for some happy passerby. That I can live in this enormous Ocean of Unknowing, not in fear but in gratitude. Not to plunder, but to tend. Not to shape it into something else, but to be shaped by it. Whatever your religion—even none—Earth is the sanctuary and we are the celebrants.

Predict-Me-Not

I waited for a bus yesterday that arrived thirteen minutes behind schedule. Standing there gazing up the boulevard, checking my watch every thirty seconds, I slowly drove myself nuts. Meanwhile, a teenager stood beside me with ear buds and most definitely not a care in the world. We shared that space, that waiting space, but while I wrung my hands like Woody Allen, she just swayed to the music in her private world.

I wonder sometimes where I got the penchant to keep the world on time and so ordered in its doings. Where things happen as they should. You know exactly what I mean: the books balance and the laundry gets done. The dogs come when they are called and the mole sauce has just the right amount of cumin. People open doors for one another, and the borrowed tool comes back. Buses, people and sunrises all arrive on schedule. Can my world have a little surprise now and again? Sure, but send it to me in moderation please, a twist of lemon in my water, or possibly the way the pool feels cold but only when I first jump in. I have a partiality for a world where challenges create wins for us and not replacements. Where routine keeps us all cool headed. All is calm, all is bright, all the freaking time. Heck, never mind the big picture. Right now I just want to buy piglets. Where are they? I've looked high and low. Seems no one has pigs for sale any more. I've been searching and waiting far more than thirteen minutes past the time when I am supposed to have those little guys. And as I stare up Pig Boulevard, I still don't see them coming.

Of course, the folly of my grey-scaled Pleasantville world is unavoidably colourized by the actual world. The real one that often flattens with one strong blast all predictability and calm. Yes, the sun will rise tomorrow on time. But after that, let's face it, it's anything goes. The world—Life—is the spinning top, the smirking imp, the Mt. St. Helens. Unfettered and a little crazy. Busting out of a box. Spiking the punch. Streaking naked across the sky. This world is a teacher that does not lecture but shows. For those with eyes and ears the lessons are clear: Be supple. Adapt. Do not clutch onto things. Get less concerned about the outcomes. And most of all, when thwarted, be ready for something that just might be better.

Yes, on that last bit, next week the sheep arrive. If you have been to our farm you will know that we have acres of inherited grass here, and the tidy world of my making means that I must regularly sit my derrière down on a ride on mower to cut it all nice and neat. So bring on the sheep. Something better is on the way.

Mementos for Amnesiacs

Sitting on my desk is an old tack hammer that belonged to my grandfather. At the turn of the last century he apprenticed as a buggy trimmer, and later made the transition to Model T's. I like to keep that hammer close. It's a 'roots' thing, of course. My ancestors were singularly people of little means: a sharecropper, a garment factory worker, a carpenter, a clerk. I like to remember my bloodlines. I like to remember that Grandpa had no formal education after the sixth grade, but put a tool in his hand, and he was a genius, a master of his craft, a Rhodes Scholar of matchless skill. I still wag my head disbelieving, in pure admiration at what Grandpa could do.

As we explore what it is to farm again, I often say that "sometimes the way forward is to look back." Back, that is, to before the time when heavy equipment crushed down the soil. Before farms, in the name of food, effectively became dumping sites for poisonous chemicals. Before monoculture cropping narrowed the otherwise rich variety of our food, and then fashioned what little was left into something perfectly shaped, perfectly presented, and yet perfectly tasteless.

We need to get restored, with sensible farming and healthy food. We need to find our way back, so that we can again go forward. Admittedly, we have some amnesia. Secrets near lost. How did Grandma pickle those beans? How did Grandpa build that chair? On our farm I discovered an old smokehouse buried under brambles in a stand of hemlock. I rebuilt it, not knowing, but asking. "Why just here? Why is the fire pit below grade? Are those the vestiges of cedar racks I see? Ah! They vented it on two opposite sides, so I shall do the same." The past spoke, and because it did, we now have smoked ham.

Once we are tutored by our elders past, we can then move thoughtfully forward with the best knowledge of today for, of course, the best of both are needed. In farming. In life. And if someday our grandchildren have a memento kept near, then we will know that we also became geniuses in our time.

Predict-Me-Not, the Sequel

Recently I contemplated the importance of being supple. I wish to say more. Because near to the greenhouse there is a certain apple tree, and it is dying. Perhaps the land is too wet there, or the soil too acidic, or the sun too weak. But why, less than five meters away in virtually the same soil and the same sun and with every comparison being equal, does its companion flourish?

Beyond the tree I see another head scratcher. In the paddock we call "de Polder" there is a waterway that we dug last year. Before doing so, we carefully noted where the water naturally wanted to flow. Simple. This one was so obvious. And that's exactly where we dug. Why then does the water now want to drift elsewhere?

We make our plans, but our plans are often frustrated. History is strewn, of course, with schemes gone askew. Think only of the world's most famous emblem of success-turned-embarrassment. They built it a few meters too close to the Arno River. *Ecco* and *poof*. (When I was a kid we called it "the leaning tower of Pizza"). Edsel. Titanic, Waterworld, wing suits and Google Glass. Donald over Hillary. The minor shah of Persia sending Genghis Khan's peace diplomat home minus his head. Decca turning down the Beatles. *Oops!*

Still, we do our utmost to force the results we desire. We tell ourselves that the consequences rest on getting just right the calculations, the foresight, the "what ifs" considered, the timing, the location. We must correctly prophesy, we must fashion the results, we must control. These are the tikis we have cached away inside us.

But there is the apple tree. Of course we had planned for it to thrive there. Instead it is dying, and I do not know why. This is the truth about farming, and about most everything else: there is always an inscrutable element or two at play, a mystery, a higher or a lower something affecting our life story. Every day we wake up to unforeseen changes, and hitches in our otherwise ordered world. Every day we encounter forces larger than ourselves.

I am keeping vigil now. A vigil is nothing else but waiting. But my urge to know rises there. I lean in to hear any word or wisdom. "Why are you dying?" I ask. I would really like to know.

Instead she whispers her last, "Hold lightly your outcomes."

Less Work, Thank You

Before I wised up, the Protestant work ethic nearly killed me. You know it: work hard, save your pennies, then work harder. Then die. This principle, and not piety alone, will redeem you. Or so it is said. Today I have a new ethic, and I say it without shame: I'm trying to find ways to do less work. There are a few methods I might consider to go about practising my new idea. One is to just get lazier. I'd like that. It sounds good on paper. And that might be possible somewhere; say, in a goofproof job where it would cost more to fire me than keep me. Or possibly, if work is more of time filler than a stomach filler (which it isn't). But on a farm this method will not fly. You can skip weeding the potatoes and they will probably give you some return anyway because, after all, tubers live mostly bombproof, hermetic lives below ground. But if you choose not to feed dozens of livestock you might end up with a scene out of Jurassic Park. No, there's no escaping a certain amount of work around here. The other method is to obtain a greater reward for the work you do. This, of course, is the smart way. How can we do less and get more? Double or triple the current return on every calorie burned, every hour clocked, every buck spent?

Once again Nature provides us with instructions. For instance, mulching around trees (as Nature does) or, better yet, introducing perennials that are symbiotic with that tree are one such way (goodbye Weed Whacker!). Another way is to ease up some on the penchant for tidy edges and other very non-Nature human obsessions for order, predictability and calm. It is actually just fine to just "let it go" here and there. "Wilding" parts of the landscape are both beautiful and provide habitat for beneficial species of birds, insects and other creatures. These, in turn, will work for you; birds, for instance, being Nature's best pesticide, while bees and dragonflies will happily pollinate the crops. Yet another is to "multi-task" plants, animals and structures. A plant may in succession or all-at-once provide shade, windbreak and food. Before an animal becomes your dinner, it can mow your grass and provide fertilizer. A structure can have one use in spring (such as propagating seeds) and another in winter (such as cold storage). The more hats we can put on various farm elements, the less work we will end up doing. Multiple functions reduces work and waste, maximizes resources, and strengthens your systems with the homerun power of Nature, diversity. Even around the house, finding and then using objects that do more than one task will save us work, money and space, and reduce our consumption. Let's find creative ways to get the real down time we deserve.

A Summer Salad Like a Rapture

"Coffee toffee." That's what Mr. Hodges called them. From across his desk my father's boss opened his hand, and with a mirthless smile that said, "*I know how much you kids love these*" offered the hard candies to his star salesman's young twin sons. In fact, Steve and I had already had to fake it once, doing what we had been taught to do: respect your elders, say thank you for a gift, and, in this specific case, put the cursed thing from your father's overlord in your mouth. Coffee toffee; ghastly things I tell you. How distinctly I remember tucking that drop against a far corner of my cheek and leaving it there as undisturbed as possible. Cyanide! Hemlock! We'd suffered through it once and now, unbelievably, we have to again. Oh the horror! Out the door at last and without a nanosecond to spare, *PTOOOEY!* Two more gruesome tasting somethings shattered on the sidewalk.

In my younger years I also felt the just the same about tomatoes. Why did anyone eat these things? They were neither sweet like Junior Mints nor savoury like Fritos. They were neither firm like a pork chop nor smooth like ice cream. Just blandish. Just pasty. Just a middling add on to an iceberg salad and Kraft Thousand Island dressing. *PTOOOEY.*

As I reminisce on my inauspicious early life with food I am sipping on a delicious morning coffee, grateful that the rank imitation Mr. Hodges foisted on us did not ruin me to the pleasure of the real thing. Nothing like a good coffee. Likewise, the salad that Dawn served up yesterday evening: heritage tomatoes, red onions, a drizzle of olive oil, and, like an erotic afterthought, a garnish of sweet Genovese Basil. Friends, it was ecstasy, and a monumental antithesis to the food world in which I was reared.

There is a simple but deep truth in the kitchen: let the food do the work. The real food, of course. Grown at home or as close to home as you can get it, from among a rich variety that industrial food does not provide, harvested ripe, and served fresh. And let the coffee toffee in all our past be damned.

De and Re Generation

Dotted across our farm are reminders of a once deeply forested land. I speak of those massive old cedar stumps, bearing witness to a not-so-distant past when the light at the ground was fully diffused, that ground carpeted more than overgrown, and when the canopy rose 250 or more feet high. Our particular site was preempted in 1890 (a polite term used to effectively expropriate land from the indigenous peoples). I sometimes imagine the land as it was then. In 1792 George Vancouver alit at what is now Chaster Creek, which flows through our farm. He had this to say of our coast: "The country produces forest trees in great abundance, of some variety and magnitude…the woods are little encumbered with bushes or trees of inferior growth."

If we wanted it back, we'd need to leave it be for five hundred years and then some. But here's the thing: those stumps have ferns, salal, huckleberries, and new cedars sprouting from them. Nature is nothing if not persistent. Her determination to green the landscape and to utterly fill it with an abundance of life and food is overpowering. We may help or hinder her, but she is *just plain unstoppable*.

Dawn and I evidenced this again yesterday on a fine evening as we sat beside one of the three ponds we dug. We sat quietly so as not to disturb the blue heron that found the water pleasant there. As do the innumerable tadpoles and their froggy parents. And the multitude of dragonflies, bees, and water spiders. The grass snakes too, and the water-loving florae. It was a scene of both wonder and quiet joy. I knew that we were both thinking the same thing, both amazed at how swiftly this diversity of life has appeared. It was Dawn who broke the silence when she wryly said for us both, "You build it and they will come."

But what did we build? We merely dug some large holes, albeit strategically, to capture and store a most precious resource. Then we sat in the grandstands and cheered while Nature exerted her signature power. The power to regenerate.

BoBo Be aBarkin'

We understand that in his former life he was known as "Buddy," but he answers today to other monikers: Bodie, Mr. B., BoBo aBarkin', and because he has truly earned this one, The Ambassador. A rescue animal is a roll of the dice but Bodie is a winner in almost every way, so much so that I declared to Dawn that he was "the only good thing to ever come out of Texas" (apologies to Willie Nelson). Of course he still has certain rescue dog quirks. Take, for instance, his dog bark thing, which is largely back-asswards; barking not so much when you arrive as when you leave (is that a "Goodbye!" or a "Don't go!"?). The Ambassador is also quite fond of reaching out to strangers with a warm and welcoming, gender indiscriminate hump. Oops. Manners BoBo! Finally, being a true southerner by birth, he is also lazy as heck in the heat and, in any weather, will never stand when he can sit, or sit when he can lie down. There's a lot to like about Mr. B's lifestyle choices.

True, Mr. B. is not the brightest guy in the room. With his companion Mikayla, they make our farm dog pair, two sentries on eight acres. But it's often less guard-like and more comedy act, Mikayla the straight man and Bodie the daffy one. If a raven is looking to swipe a chicken egg, Mikayla zooms straight for it, howling, full gallop. Bo-Bo-aBarkin'—who runs just like a piglet—joins in until, inexplicably, he makes a sudden left turn while Mikayla, the raven, and the whole world, just turned right. Like a Blue Angel in slo-mo, he peels off into the mist. He just does dumb stuff like that. Then there's the looks department: Mikayla of show dog pedigree, fine boned, with a coat like silk; Mr. B. built like a shot putter with dense, lumpy fur, such that he must go to the barber twice a year. As it turns out, however, smarts and looks don't matter much. Because whatever aptitude, whatever beauty this mutt lacks is more than compensated by a singular, life-infused enthusiasm. I tell you, the guy is flat out happy.

But it was not always this way. When we first got Bo he had clearly been living in some form of Hell. His head hung, his tail hung. He had no energy. He was hurting. He could not even climb stairs. Most of all, as we would come to discover, he was hiding his personality. Bodie had learned to survive by being invisible.

Then he caught his break. He went from whatever confined space he inhabited to a lush, generous land with curiosities unnumbered on it. Here he is affirmed. Here he is respected for what he is. He is fed and groomed and scratched and cuddled. Bodie is born again.

What's not to love about this old guy? And aside from the run like a piglet, what's not to emulate? The past can never be swept clean forever, but just a little love our way, and I feel certain that we can be healed of our broken spirit, and possibly even of our broken body. So then, a small reminder here of an everyday truth: if love comes our way, a little affirmation here, a little scratch and cuddle there, let's take it. It is exactly what we need.

Carpe Momentum

Dawn dropped a large container in front of me and announced "These are the best of the very best, and it looks like the last of them also." I saw them: perfect in shape and size, deep with ripened colour, and then...the aroma. It wafted up to me like incense. I put one into my mouth, and went fleetingly hallucinogenic with the wild rush of flavor.

The very best. We ate a whole bowlful then, and though they didn't need it, we festooned them with whipped cream and a drizzle of chocolate. It was a moment of glory, and a moment of melancholy also. For how could it be that the best is the last, and that the last is already?

A strawberry. A glory. A broccoli spear. A glory. A snap pea, a tomato, a persimmon, a cucumber, a leaf of cilantro. A blade of grass, a note of music floating, a laugh, a sunset, a love for you and a love for me. Glories all. Every day on a farm (and every day in every walk of life) we are counselled to revel in that moment of ripeness, in the apogee of aliveness, when Chronos (sequential time) suddenly transfigures into Kairos (momentous time), into that exact moment that is 'best.'

Let us revel friends, for when we next blink, the moment will be gone.

The Be-Attitudes

There are days when I have to wonder why. The animals begin their canonical hours before daybreak, chanting for breakfast. We may not have slept much the night before but did any of these say, "Ah! Sleep in then, and I'll bring you coffee at nine." Nah. When the dew burns off Dawn and I have already been at it for an hour or more. Any of a hundred tasks need attention, and which few get done is determined by a push-me pull-you dance between urgency and randomness. It may be seeding or laying row cover, moving mulch or pruning tomatoes, repairing the greenhouse or shoveling manure. If not these, there is always the endless battle with our crop's competition. "Organic!" I sputter. "Must be Latin for 'eternal weeding.'" I wrestle out another Dock Weed; it has a tap root like Rebar. I see my hands, miraculous appendages so doted on by their owners in every culture and in every age. And guess what? They look horrible.

By midday the sun is a sledgehammer. In a lapse of altruism I think, "Those poor little piggies! I will top up their wallow so they may enjoy an afternoon mud bath." But once there I discover that the Tamworth has broken through the fence again. Hear me now: We give these bacon an entire acre to live on, but they are nothing if not porcine capitalists: they want the entire seven others. Of course, chasing down a Tamworth is a fool's game. A pig can break and dodge better than any halfback. The Tamworth knows this fact also, and because she does, she simply smiles, maliciously, and then munches on a broccoli plant. That is to say, munching on our profit.

I go next to check the farmstand. Who can solve the mystery of why, when the weather is hot, sales go into a deep freeze? Then the light bulb goes on: Mystery solved! The local supermarket has air conditioning. Then the light bulb goes off, when I wonder whether I should install a swamp cooler on the farmstand.

The day marches to its end, almost. The neighbor lost two sheep last week to a cougar, and though it is approaching the dinner hour, we just found one. Or rather, it found us, when the afternoon wind turned and the sickening odor wafted into the kitchen. I wade into a thicket and find the carcass, a swollen, teeming mass of maggots. It's too deep and too disgusting in there to pull it out, so I bushwhack back in with a sack of lime, a jerry rigged extreme unction. Appetite now on hold, I go for a G and T instead.

"How was your day?" I ask Dawn. "God it was hot," she says, "but did you hear how happy the animals were this morning? How they just give glory for the new day? I got so much done too. Three rows in Elysium Field have been weeded and prepped for fall. Weeding is such a peaceful activity. You get to be all alone with your thoughts!" Ah Dawn, she of the predictably sunny mind. "By the way I saw the Tamworth out again. She's such a sucker for a little grain, comes full clip right back home. What else? Oh, get this! Somebody left a beautiful note at the farmstand today. They spent thirty-two bucks, but left a fifty dollar bill, and thanked us for doing what we do. How cool is that?!" Obtuse and reticent to leave my sullenness I ask, "Cool like a swamp cooler?" "Huh?" she says, then like a skipping stone she races on. "To think that I could still be stuck in some awful job."

I take another sip on my drink. Feels good, how it cools me on the inside. Give me a minute here.

Fine then, maybe Dawn has a point.

Living On the Edges

Fernando and I walked the land. This is the custom. Before discussions about wayward sons or high taxes or that uncomfortable procedure you had, you walk the land together. Talk some about what is growing. Observe the lessons. We stopped to see the progress on his onions. We noted the pasture grass buttressing the contours, the furrows wending with the landscape. Fernando looked out, and without turning, said, "We want our furrows to be straight, like the furrows in our minds, which are always so." He paused long enough for me to consider the awful consequences of furrows running straight up and over the crest of hills. In that land of blistering sun and torrential rain I did not have to consider long. "But in the country the lines are always curved." He turned to me then. "To follow the shape of the land is *muy importante*."

Muy importante indeed. Since Fernando's lesson long ago, I have become a full time curve devotee. I like curves on people. I like them on furniture. I like them in the garden. I even like them in baseball (sometimes). Curves are the preferred method of Nature. They are everywhere. Curves make for more edges, which make for more interesting opportunities. Get down low, close to the sidewalk, and have a look at the edge. There's more going on there, isn't there? It is a little greener, has a few different plants trying things out. More insects too. Edges are always more dynamic places, small little climate zones that join one system to another and, while creating their own edge ecosystem, stimulate more variety which in turn, creates more resilience. If you are fashioning a new garden, or putting in a new footpath, or digging a pond, toss in lots of squiggly edges. Edges make for greater variety, and variety is the key to a healthy and interesting garden. Come to think of it, of a healthy and interesting life too.

The Ground of Our Being

I love a good talk on the nature of things, the 'what and the why' of the world, the role of people in the world, and the more prickly questions of the unseen but real. Metaphysics. Ontology. Epistemology. Existence. Reason. Universe. Nature. That kind of stuff.

Oh shoot! Did I lose you already? Did you suddenly have chill memories of a skinny old bespectacled prof with unkempt white hair and a monotone drone? Of all that impenetrable philosophy-speak, with its spaghetti-like conversation that can get you lost faster than you can get yourself lost on an L.A. freeway? Well, I don't blame you. So let me bring you back, and quickly, with this claim: no word in the English language has been so waylaid and left for dead as the word "philosophy," which, easily parsed, means simply, "the love of wisdom."

Let's start again then, shall we? Existence. The love of wisdom. The Universe. The love of wisdom. Nature. The love of wisdom. Reasoning. The love of wisdom. Conduct. The love of wisdom. Knowledge. The love of wisdom. The meaning of Life. The love of wisdom. I realize, of course, that I can't blame the English language for the appropriation of philosophy. Heck, it was the Greeks themselves who started it all, declaring value in the pursuit of knowledge 'for its own sake.' From the get-go philosophy began earning its reputation for being damnably abstract, puttering about intellectually with great self absorption, but having little to actually do with life on the ground, with whether you will stop on red, or pay the new price on a pint of Häagen Dazs or even if you will enlist to become a sniper in Iraq. But what began in Greece seems to have been perfected by our modern institutions, where most all of our learning comes by reflection and almost not at all by experimentation. In fact, I used to call my student days, "life in a book-lined bomb shelter."

Well, I admit I always feel refreshed after I have vented a bit on academia. Still, academia or not, there are powerful, intriguing, and needful questions that humans regularly find themselves asking. Am I part of a larger design? Do I have any duty to the Earth? Who is my neighbour? How do I know that what I know is what I need to know? Is it okay to be me? Is there a God, or a 'something' to which I belong? In a world where we are defined by what we do, what does it mean to 'be'?

It is not exactly a pushover to make such questions more connected to our real world, everyday lives, but I do have this to say: The love of wisdom. Can we get back to this please? By definition, wisdom is "knowledge, experience, and good judgment." It's not hard to love those qualities at all! Together they are formidable in their world changing power. Hence, true philosophy embraces learning as an adventure in the world, right down in the mud, the blood and the beer of it all, in such a manner that reason, spirituality, and ethics actually do affect whether we stop on red. True philosophy is learned when we grab a fistful of soil, when we feel the wind sweeping down Elphinstone mountain, or feast together at a pot luck. We hear it teach us in wordless Nature, and coax us in the engine that will not start until we fix it. We see it budding in the seedling that rises strong, thanks to our collaborative work in co-creating. Love of wisdom is our foundation. It is the ground beneath our feet, the ground behind and before us. It is the ground of our very being.

Make Hay

Kudos to the Romney sheep for doing their best to keep me off the ride on mower. But the truth is, even our food-fixated ruminants can't keep up with the grass this time of year. So it came time to hitch up the flail mower to the John Deere. Now, think not merely 'next step up from a ride on mower' here. Unlike the ride on, the flail mower is not built to give you the droll feeling of buzzing about in a little go-Kart. It is not fitted with a cup holder on the side for your beer, and it's probably best not to listen to music with your headset on while using it. In short, it is one serious piece of equipment. Because ours matches the tractor (that is, old and crotchety) it's a maddening job to hitch up. We went at it, Dawn sportingly providing help while I spat and cursed. But once on, the job was fast: I had the whole Brookbank savannah whacked down in little more than an hour. Done and done.

And then the past spoke. Or rather, the past leapt out at me when I remembered a few old photographs I have. Taken sometime in the Thirties of Brookbank Farm, one of them shows two men and a draft horse gathering hay. Yes, in that time when a homestead grew food not only for humans but also food for animals. *Doh!* And to think that Dawn had just returned from the feed store with a bale of hay that busted thirty bucks! It was nothing to let the good sun bake the cut grass, and little effort on our part to turn it once or twice, and to gather it up. Now we have got some nice hay to last us awhile. I almost missed an easy opportunity.

'Make hay while the sun shines' says the old proverb. Sometimes I simply miss that chance, that opening, even though is right in front of me, and its 'easy pickings.' Forbid me that I should start sounding like a horoscope just now, but is it not true that we all need to exploit opportunities to our advantage? To make some hay! And to do it while the sun shines, because of course, it does not shine every day.

C'mon Clouds. You Can Do It

For the glory, for the pure gratitude of it, no shower in my entire life has yet to compare to the one I once had in a decrepit hotel room in St. Louis, Senegal. A modest trickle of tepid and murky water was all it was, but as I stooped a little to get under it, heaven came down on me. Somewhere in that eternity of bliss I soaped myself and then watched with fascination as the weeks of hard, hot travel, the caked on dirt of Spanish Sahara and Mauritania, yielded itself, circled slowly at my feet, and disappeared down the drain. I will never forget what a little water in Africa did for me then.

Fast forward forty plus years. I gaze down into our ponds at Brookbank Farm. Or rather, I gaze into the three enormous holes where ponds are supposed to be. Where are the 200,000 liters of water we have stored there? There's some sludgy-ick left, is all. It's not quite mid August and the land is withered. In our province and beyond, fires are busting out everywhere. The term 'global warming' is being batted around in talk shows and at dinner tables everywhere. Here on the Coast where we receive rainforest level annual precipitation the argument about who's to blame for our water shortage is so recurrent in the weekly newspaper it should be a permanent part of the masthead.

Against solving the growing crisis of a desiccating world we have only two adversaries. The first is illiteracy. I am a firm believer that knowledge frees (even if that knowledge is at first difficult to admit). As to our appreciation of water, there is no end to educating ourselves, and to respectfully passing on our knowledge. The second adversary is our memory loss. Come November, when we are soggy again and frustrated with all the water everywhere, searing heat and dusty lawns are not so present in our thinking. Let each of us then remember our Africa. Remember that time, place, event, when the water mattered to you. Possibly when it saved you.

Last night the clouds rolled in and while nothing has fallen yet, we have our fingers crossed. I'll bet you do also. I'll bet that we can remember this feeling we have right now, somewhere past November.

The Low Hanging Fruit

At the supermarket there's an entire aisle of quasi-food ("snacks") dedicated to a scientific truth: human evolution is such that we naturally crave salt, fat, and sugar. (My own scientific truth adds to that list; expensive, shiny new toys, massive recognition, and a back rub that possibly leads to other things, but I'll save that for another time). I must be still crawling out of the primordial soup myself, because I'm largely a single-crave creature: sugar. I have such tender memories of wheedling a dime off my mother and heading straight to the Village Market with it, there to plumb the Gnostic depths of the longest, most beautiful candy counter ever created. What should I get this time? The perfectly created Crunch bar? A box of Milk Duds because they stick to the roof of my mouth? Or something sassy perhaps, like Necco or Red Hots? In North America sugar consumption rose from an average of three kilos annually per person in 1900 to over fifty kilos per person in 2000. Well folks, for Evolution of the Sapien sweet tooth, and for the Motherland, I certainly did my part. Cookies, Cokes and Frosted Flakes. Gum, ice cream and Cracker Jack. Oh yes, and fruit too! Pulverized, reconstituted, shot through with food colour, corn starch, and more sugar, and sent back to me as a delectable little Hostess Pie.

I'll skip the story of my own long, sometimes tortured, sometimes still-faulty, journey away from non-food crap and go right to the good ending. The good ending isn't about me. The good ending is in the accompanying photograph. Yes, that gaggle of kids you see there, two of them my grandkids, who took part—or rather, *could not be restrained*—from picking the-low-hanging-fruit-of-the-Earth-as-manifest-in-apples. We had a great time. On at least two counts it was another eye opener for me.

First, I saw an ancient tree as a long candy counter. While a sugar crave may be hardwired into humans, a Crunch bar isn't. I was joyed to watch children gorge on Nature's provision (and I was grateful to their parents). In fact, Nature deftly provides a veritable procession of sweetness through most of the year. Strawberries and other early berries, both domestic and wild. Cherries next, and when these fade the plums arrive. Midsummer brings currants, thimbleberries and blueberries. August is here with apples, sundry melons, and blackberries. In September there will be pears, grapes, crab apples, and cranberries. In the colder months we can reach for the same food that we preserved in advance.

Second, I saw my teachers again. I mean the kids, of course, the little Yodas all around us, who have not yet been sullied by adult refinements. Who are still unpretentious and who thrill in simple pleasures. Who live on the surface, say what they see, and most of all, *who naturally gravitate to goodness.* Hence, they lead us back to where we need to be. Back to the low hanging fruit in life. There to pluck the uncomplicated delight, there to sink teeth and heart into wholeness. Back to the easy sugar.

K.I.S.S. (Keep It Simple Sage)

This is a month of abundance. The bears know this fact. They are everywhere now, feasting themselves with single minded abandon. It's a full scale pig out: plants, fruits, nuts, insects, honey, fish, small mammals and carrion. I've sighted six of our ursine friends in the last week alone, including a massive one that wandered through our farm yesterday. Easily busting over 300 pounds, he shambled by like the Lord of the Manor. Not a care in the world. A bona fide Balloo Incarnate he was. You remember Balloo, of course, creation first of Kipling and latterly of Disney. In the animation, Balloo effortlessly popped open ripe coconuts and ass-bumped banana trees to jiggle off the fruit. He wriggled his fulsome bottom and sang pure wisdom:

Look for the bare necessities
The simple bare necessities
Forget about your worries and your strife
I mean the bare necessities
Old mother nature's recipes
That bring the bare necessities of life.

It may seem incongruous that the merits of simplicity are lauded in the time of greatest abundance. Or not. For what better time to consider them than the time when you need them the least? What better time to gain your sovereignty over fears of scarcity and need? Whether in plenty or in want, simplicity is the better path to joy.

I was eleven years old when Balloo first sashayed across the silver screen singing. If only I would have heard, I mean really heard, his music away back then.

Don't spend your time lookin' around
For something you want that can't be found
When you find out you can live without it
And go along not thinkin' about it
I'll tell you something true
The bare necessities of life will come to you

So, you might say, it is to the life of a chicken that I now aspire. Because I wish to live more simply. To find ways to unwind the tangled mess of my emotions. To speak from a place of humility, with a listening ear, what my truth is, as I understand it. Sometimes I will be afraid, because my constructs are so large and so looming. But I am going to do my best to stare down that tower of doom. Because I wish to be healed, and to see others around me healed as well. And because the surface is where the good food, and the good sunshine, are.

The Unseen Real

We walk in the forest, Mikayla and I. There are few forests in the world as inspiring as those of the Pacific Northwest. Cedar and fir trees rise twenty and more stories high. Even the hemlocks tower above. My eyes are always drawn upward by those impossibly long vertical lines. I take in the wonder of those great trees and the green canopy of abundance above. I love what I see. I can't *believe* what I see. The prisms of colour. The vaulted ceilings. The sense that just up there and beyond is a threshold to another world. Is the forest not the original cathedral? Small wonder that my spirit is elevated there.

Mikayla, on the other hand, is grooving on other things. Sure, she may look up to watch a bird sail past, but otherwise her face is being pulled to the forest floor—that is to say, *in the opposite direction that mine is*—where she is having her own form of spiritual rush. Because while my paltry five million or so scent receptors work to process whether that is cedar I smell or my new deodorant, Mikayla's 200 million plus receptors are feasting on a banquet of specific and highly diverse information in that same forest. So there it is. I with my eyes upward, in my ecstasy. My dog with her nose downward, in an ecstasy of her own. We share the same sacred space, but Mikayla's forest experience is totally different than mine.

What I mean to say is that there is a whole other reality out there that I know nothing about. This is astonishing to me, that there should be two parallel worlds, and doubly so because if Mikayla did not confirm to me her world is there, it would be completely unknown to me. So many are the implications of this simple truth, I might contemplate a lifetime on them.

This juxtaposed, interconnected, two-or-more-world-wonder is no less astonishing in a food garden. To grow anything in fact is to embrace the humbling truth that while we apply our best knowledge to succeed, we also rely every moment on certain mysteries to do what they do. The hair trigger in the seed. The bustling microbial community in the soil. The secret light factory that churns out biomass. The cargo ship pollinators. The fountain of life in a dewdrop. This immense, organized and articulate world of 'otherness' somehow meets ours; there is a convergence, and the result is the miracle of food. It is thrilling and chastening both, to straddle the worlds, and to feast joyfully on the outcome. Ah, but I see that it's time now to leave the sacred for the profane again. Or not. For said mutt is presently giving me the look that surely translates the same in every world: "Let's go out for another see/smell reverence/walk!"

To Do

File taxes (late). Build wattle fence. Clear deadfall. Repair gutters. Plant fall crops. Organize workshop. Mulch new herb garden. Pay bills. Clean chicken coop. Fix water pipe. Patch fence. Complete documentation report. Service rototiller. Dry oregano. Prep farm collective boxes...and for the love of God, vacuum. The list is endless sometimes, and just staying ahead on it, much less *shortening* it feels like a pipe dream.

We all live busy and complex lives. Managing our time and just getting most things done when they need to get done seems not only to drive us, but to define us. Do this routine long enough and we begin to measure ourselves less on creativity and on the now almost forgotten 'joy factor', and more on outputs and production. Bing bang bong and fiddle dee dee.

Until, that is, we get broadsided. It took a recent hospital experience and now subsequent season of recuperation to help me realize again two fundamental truths. First, forget all that complicated, urgent, and weighty stuff on your never ending 'To Do' list. Instead, revel in the everyday gifts that often go unnoticed. I feel hot water cascading down my body again. I see a welcome wag from the dogs. I can pee again, and walk again, however wobbly. I can cast my eyes on this good land and feast on the visual banquet that is the burgeoning season all around me. The food growing. The piglet sunning. The soft wind in the trees. Second, I realize that, in the end, creativity and joy will always outshine outputs and production. Bing bang bong, look what I did! As a child of my culture and times, I had embedded in me the importance of outputs. So let me say this unambiguously, a declaration of intent: 'To Do' lists, go take a hike. And that is no small intent, because of course slowing down, even if only for a stated season, does not come easily. To be ready to discover new dimensions of life in that place of slowness will be nothing less than a spiritual journey for me.

So I begin now, with a 'thank you' not for the things done, but for the things that simply are: the flowering apple tree, the clack of the raven in the cedar, the embrace of my partner, and the moment when your whisper carries across the land.

We of the Larger Brain

On the grand stage of planet Earth, diversity reigns supreme. However, it is equally true that species gather and herd to themselves. It's just natural. For reproductive reasons, for protection, for the social life of that species, birds, mammals, fish, insects, and even some reptiles simply hang out with their own. And we of the 'larger brain' species are hardly different. We also gravitate to homogeneity, be it for similar interests or social status or ethnic heritage or spirituality or politics. When we bunch together our specific interest is reinforced, our protection is assured, and our ideology is defended. What's not to like?

I will tell you what's not to like. A bomb in a subway is what's not to like. Concentration camps, lynchings, hate rallies, and classism are what's not to like. Injustice over your own back fence is what's not to like. Hegemony on a grand scale is what's not to like. Profiteering is what's not to like. Degradation of the planet is what's not to like. Any human thinking himself better than any other human is what's not to like.

We of the larger brain, we that walk upright, we with vast expression of thought and emotion through language, we of the *imago Dei*, we that can reach so high and yet still tumble so low, we are in great need just now of seeing past the immediate pull to homogeneity.

For beside the clustering of the species, there is another and equally cogent lesson. Shouted just as loud from every treetop, in every streamlet, under every stone, by every creature, is the crucial interplay of species. They have learned to cross the divide, in order to form mutually beneficial relationships. They are distinct and yet codependent. They go about the madcap business of continuing their own, and yet at the same moment serve the needs of another. They have learned that diversity is an act of necessity equal to or greater than homogeneity. I mean just that: a crucial, biological necessity. And, perhaps not shouted but spoken everywhere and loud enough to hear, they have learned that diversity is an expression of a certain genius, and therefore an act of celebration.

Make It Beautiful

It is the lie of the land, how it slopes ever so gently to the southwest. It is the natural revegetation taking place, those salmon berries and alders and hemlock and cedar. It is the fields fully productive now and the fruit trees hanging low. It is the Great Hall, our no-touch forest zone with Chaster Creek running through it. There are so many places here, so many corners and nooks, to cast an appreciative eye. This is Brookbank, our beloved land. Where Nature is the artist, creating masterpieces.

And we are Nature's apprentices. When we put our brush to this canvas, we employ principles that we learn from the master. Chief among these is variety. There is also multiple functions, energy efficiency, layers, plant succession, and not least, eye popping beauty.

Not long after moving to Brookbank, Dawn and I put set ourselves to work to create a doorstep garden. More exactly, I did what I call "the Jethro part," moving earth and setting bricks and building a deck, while Dawn, who is far more advanced as an apprentice of Nature than I, put her talent on display with an exquisite palette of colour, shape, size, and function. We often sit on the front deck now as evening approaches. Before us the garden is maturing (at our arrival it was only a misplaced rhododendron and more of the ubiquitous lawn). Yesterday I saw this garden with new eyes. Simply said, it is beautiful. It simultaneously soothes and fascinates me. An extra curvy brick path that leads to a gated arbour makes for a pleasing look and extra edges. A rich diversity of plantings, both food and ornamental, create a rainbow of colours, shapes, layers, and functions. Lavender, hollyhock, thyme, and asparagus form an attractive perimeter. An herb spiral draws the eye yet higher. There is both a 'wildness' to the garden, and yet also a design. I really love it, and by the way so do the great legions of honey bees and other pollinators.

Nature provides us both the model and the materials to co-create something beautiful. Wherever you garden, wherever you live, wherever you breathe, add the aesthetics. Make it diverse, and make it beautiful.

Sector Surrender

A rich, loamy earth is a thing of beauty. But farming is not only about what's in the soil. There are many influences on the land that are not fixed to the land. In the *lingua franca* of permaculture practice we call these "sectors." Tops on the list of sectors, of course, are sun, wind, and water. But there are many others; for instance, people, animal, bird and other creaturely movement, noise, frost, and lightning. Politics, social trends, and bylaws are all invisible, but they also deeply influence our land. Earthquakes come and go, but they might create a canyon on your back forty where one never was.

A sector is always a head scratcher. Do we want it here? Can we get more of it? Or do we not want it? Can we prevent it from entering? Or perhaps we want it, but differently than it now is. You can alter the influence of full sun merely by plopping a baseball cap on your head. If you need more shade than that, you can erect structures, or plant trees for dapple light. Likewise, water is generally a welcome sector, but if it's pounding down on your tomatoes or running across your driveway, you may want to attempt to channel it. Here at Brookbank Farm, for instance, we channeled the water energy sector with our ponds and waterways development. To add to the conundrums, at times a sector may be wanted, and at other times not.

The game of sectors is a particularly dicey one, for the simple reason that we are not omnipotent. In the last week or two I curtailed all physical activity and, at length, had to settle myself into a state of resignation, all for two sectors that I had no power to influence. Truly, I wish I could say that I got "zen," but it really was more akin to simple misery. I coughed. I wheezed. I dosed myself on pharmaceuticals. I speak first, of course, of the pervasive, inescapable, sector of air pollution we have had due to forest fire smoke. Second, there was an almost complete absence of any wind sector. Did you notice that the smoke drifted but did not blow? When a particulate is two microns in length (that's two millionths of a meter) there is not a lot that can be done about not breathing it. When the wind goes still you can only wait out the doldrums. The insidious Slow Death Fog would stay until either fires were quenched or the most welcome sector of wind returned. Yesterday the wind returned, albeit slightly, to clear the atmosphere. And as I resume a life of normalcy (to the extent I may be accused of such) I think retrospectively on the *powerlessness* of that experience. We do what we can to influence the influences. But we are not omnipotent.

Nice Package Is No Package

When I was a kid we hauled it to a place called Coyote Canyon. Well, that canyon filled up. So another canyon was chosen, and we went to that one. And after that one filled, another. I remember marveling that a *canyon* could actually be filled up. How is it possible to fill up a whole valley? It's possible by tossing everything into a trash can. I mean everything. And then every Tuesday, drag the large metal cans to the curb. Watch the reeking, fetid mass of bottles, food scraps, cans, paper, plastic and rubber tipped into the equally reeking truck. Watch it all get squished forward. Watch the truck crawl up the street, one house after another. All the way to Coyote Canyon. We're still paying for the destructive consumption patterns of that past time, when everything, just everything, got tossed.

Gratefully, we've made some progress since then. I say 'some', as evidenced by my journey today to the Sechelt Landfill and which makes for two distinct Pauls: the Paul who nods appreciatively at the orderliness of it all, of the segregation for recycling of wood, metal, doors and windows, paint, and of that Free Items shed for anything at all that the consumer might think someone else could use. The other Paul sees those plastic bags caught by the wind and sent helter skelter high into the neighbouring trees, macabre drapings like a demented Christmas. And those noble bald eagles—dozens of them—stooping in their excellence to pick from the human detritus. And most of all, and even after all the assiduous work to recycle, the *still perfectly useful stuff I see* down there in that great bin next to me, just out of reach and yes, still on its way to filling a canyon.

We're getting better. But let's stay at it. Find a strategy to use stuff longer, and repurpose just about everything. Flip upside down our cultural conditioning: spurn the showy, the new, and the sparkling; admire something reborn. And let's keep putting our money in the right places, purchasing goods that are not over packaged.

The profound mystery of Earth, sea, and sky is their near perfect ability to self-regenerate. Whatever we do to these harmfully, I believe, will evolve and heal with time.

But why would we harm our home? Why would we fill another canyon?

The (under)Graduate

The man is swirling his drink and talking about something. I'm nodding politely. But I've stopped listening because he's morphed into his third or fourth subject without pause and—surprise surprise—he just happens to be an expert in every one of them. I glance about, looking for my spouse-as-rescue. Heck, looking for just anyone, anything, to get me anywhere but where I am. Then a pang of shame hits me. I am being judgmental. Obviously the guy is insecure. Dying to show me he's well read, funny, and chock-a-block with world experience. He goes on and on, and next I muse on what his compelling inner demon might be. Middle of the birth order in a large family? Late bloomer got picked on in high school? Stern father, diffident mother? Something like that.

Not coincidentally, the shame I feel vanishes when I reach the limit of my patience. Hell, didn't we all get handed an imperfect childhood? Isn't his life proceeding at the same speed as the rest of us? He's salt and pepper gray, got a pot belly now...and he's still trying to convince the world that he really matters. *Of course he does*, even with all his evident needs, he matters. But his personal enlightenment seems late in coming. And *tant pis*, today is not my day for handing out revelations. So while he draws in a breath I time perfectly my out: "Man, I need to go raid those appies!"

Of course my dismissiveness is no better than his fragmented ego. I too am a work in progress. But honestly? I'm grateful that whatever insecurities I have don't add up to omniscience. Because it seems to me that the single greatest adversary of our life is the false sense that we have "arrived," that we've graduated now and got the degree, that we are no longer a student, no longer a wide-eyed, puzzled, fascinated, scared but go-forward human vessel waiting to be wowed by our next encounter with wonder. I can't put this too strongly: the secret of being at once human *and alive* is knowing that we never arrive. A man may plaster his walls from floor to ceiling with degrees, certificates, trophies, photos of victories, and sundry other recognitions. Doesn't matter. He has not arrived.

At Brookbank we have a once-a-month Volunteer Farm Day Program. We gather to work as a way to learn. I absolutely love it. Tons of needful stuff gets done that Dawn and I could never get done alone. But the reason I really love it is this: the people who come are precisely not the guy at the party. Instead they are the wide-eyed apprentices of life. They are grooving on doing and learning something new, and I can see that they will be grooving like that until their dying breath. I'm not musing on their inner demon. I'm not trying to get away from them. I'm trying to get closer! The air that circles around Life Learners is so refreshing, so crisp, so joyful. And though at day's end we are dirty and tired, it is as though we just stepped beneath a cold waterfall. Because we have been wowed all over again.

Corny Ain't So Bad

My childhood was spent in a modest town in southern California. The town grew up about the time I did, but for some years there it wasn't much. There was a movie theatre built in the Art Deco years, and a Saber jet in the public park that we kids could climb on. Fittingly, our talkative local barber held the office of mayor. We also had our once-yearly community celebration. It was called "The Fish Fry." The town was not beside any water, and I never ever saw a single fish fried (though there *must* have been), but there were other dazzling attractions. A travelling carnival took our dimes in exchange for nauseating us with whirligig rides, and beside the midway vendors of kitchen gizmos temporarily wowed our Moms. The big event however was the parade. We all lined the edges of Harbor Street to watch Cub Scouts travel by like schools of blue fish, gasp as old men wearing Fez hats did death-defying figure eights on mini bikes, and grimace as the high school marching band brought it all to a climax with another doleful Oompah tune.

Guess what? I loved it. Everybody loved it. It was simple pleasure. It brought neighbours together in the days of summer, to put aside hoes and shovels to celebrate what they had together. Food. Art. Kids. Kindness. Commerce. Earth. Sky. Water. Acceptance. Validity. Reverence.

That was a long time ago. But despite a vastly changed world, the annual Fish Fry is still going strong in my boyhood town (yes, I Googled it, seventy-one years and counting). Despite an entire new generation of world travelling, app-dependent people, the Fish Fry still has a carnival, and it still has a parade. Some things are near timeless. So much like the synergy of Nature working, where there are no solitary anythings, the best of who we are and the best of what we achieve is invariably a product of labouring, of laughing, of loving, and of simply *being* together. I hope there are Fish Fries forever, across the land.

A Wallet Awakening

So it is happening, just as so many said it would. In our local supermarkets the real price of fresh food is at last starting to surface. I overheard evidence of the reckoning last week, when a customer beside me stared into the broccoli crowns and, in a disbelieving voice, said to no one in particular, "Six dollars for that?"

Coast to Coast and beyond. California. Florida. Mexico. We laced the landscape with highways. We bribed farmers with subsidies and tax credits to grow monoculture crops, and to grow lots of them. We even bribed the plants. With post war surpluses of chemical nitrogen and phosphate wantonly applied, they leapt to a sudden and unnatural greening. Everything moving. Everything growing. At times too much. Enter "market stability" and now farmers were paid to let their peaches rot, while surpluses of butter were sold overseas for a tenth of store prices at home.

But times were too heady, and we were too busy moving. Landscapes now crisscrossed, we next laced the skies with contrails. We sent jumbo jets to fetch us tomatoes from Chili, coconuts from Thailand, and onions from China. Thus we have feasted, and thus we have grown accustomed to eat any food at any time in every place.

But now the price of broccoli has skyrocketed, and just as the price of oil has fallen. Meaning that "peak oil" is not even necessary to demonstrate how precarious our food system is. Shifting politics and social unrest. A falling currency. Drought in California. A war here, a tsunami there. It is all so volatile, this madness of motion that puts fresh strawberries on our crêpes in December.

Local food is always the smarter choice, and now that the money argument is being silenced, there is no reason left not to support the farmer nearest you. Broccoli, grown organically in your own neighbourhood, is healthier, tastier, and now with the lacework of highways and contrails unraveling, it will also be a bargain.

My Redundancy Draweth Near

Every niche in society does it. In lieu of crude truths we speak euphemisms. For instance, we do not say outright much anymore that someone has "died." That's too blunt, too unsympathetic by half. Instead we say they "passed away" or worse, "entered their rest." The military has perfected the art of not saying what they are saying. Civilians who get killed are called "collateral damage," while a well-aimed bomb is called a "surgical strike." The corporate world is another niche that uses a host of benign terms to shroud darker realities. "Correction" means the shareholders are not going to get what they signed on for. "Outsourcing" means employees at home are going to lose their job to cheap labour abroad. And anything with the word "green" in it usually means they have a creative public relations department. Yet another term is "redundant," which applies to those who found out one day that they had a doppelgänger in the company doing what they already do, making them expendable.

As to the latter, I'm hoping someday that Brookbank Farm, and me with it, becomes redundant. You heard me correctly: I want you to be my doppelgänger. Please, take my job away. You see, in the Edenic world of my mind, everyone has a garden of their own, where they grow food for themselves, plus a bit more for those who cannot.

Of course I know that for the time being I am perfectly safe from unemployment. But why not add to your diet some food of your very own? It's not so daunting to do, truly, and it does not take much time or space. Call it your Personal Victory Garden. Grow a bit, and sense your small victory over supermarket servitude! And if you are already doing it, then perhaps you could add one more corner. It is amazing the quantity and diversity of food that can be grown in the most humble of spaces.

Last week I visited my friend Eddie, where I got a sudden renewed rush of hopefulness for my own unemployment. Eddie does not have any garden space and would not want any. He is the archetypal city dwelling, career white collar worker, living in a bachelor apartment and dedicated in his free time to sports and more sports. Do you see this picture? Work, hockey, beer, more work. No, Eddie would not like to garden. But thanks to a grandma who spoiled him as a kid on the real ones, he does love tomatoes. I saw those few pots on his balcony, with those plants that needed some pruning and tying up, and Eddie beaming... and it felt like my redundancy was finally drawing near.

What Makes It Tick

Can't quite say why, but both of our vehicles have dashboard clocks that run ever so slightly slow. About once every two weeks I reset them both. Push, hold until it flashes, push, push, push. "Digital" they may be, but not so very unlike the days when, if your clock was off, you opened the front, and moved the clock hands manually to the proper time. That is to say, then and now, take the quick fix. As long as we do not get inside that clock, it won't change. It won't fix itself. Instead, we change, by developing patterns that adjust for the deficiency. By learning to live with it.

This is my somewhat offbeat introduction to say that I am done growing potatoes the way I have always grown them. Years ago, when we first started planting spuds, we encountered problems: wire worms, marginal yields, and so forth. We tinkered. Tried a few different varieties. Tried planting later, then earlier. Tried watering more, then less. Tried one location, then another. But the pattern of deficiency held, and instead of getting into the inside of the problem to create the change that would last, we changed. Dawn surrendered, but only because she is less the potato addict than I am. I soldiered on alone, but began telling myself that potatoes simply "do not grow well here." Moving the clock hands, as it were. Sure enough, this year's harvest of my beloved Sieglindes look not much different from past years.

Meantime, farmer Stephanie recently showed me her potatoes, grown right here at Brookbank, virtually right next to mine. Yep, you guessed it: they are totally gorgeous. Huh?

So it's time to step back. To observe with new eyes, then step in, but deeper. Get past the face of things, into the inner workings. Ask myself a different set of questions. Stop adjusting myself for the deficiency, content with the half-happiness of merely moving hands. Ask others for counsel. Listen to the land. Get to the core. I just happen to love potatoes, and life, that much.

The Angel Next Door

Many years ago I grew to know and love a man of extraordinary achievements, but looking at him you would never have guessed. The circumstances of his birth and early childhood had left him with daunting personal challenges. He suffered from brain damage at birth. As a child he lived with an alcoholic stepfather in mean, penniless conditions. He faltered in public school. He was clumsy with his body. He spoke with a slur. His handwriting drifted diagonally across the page. He reversed numbers, letters and words. He was tone deaf, colour blind and had almost no sense of smell. Despite these disabilities, in his lifetime he went far. He overcame, and then, in turn, dedicated himself to help others with their challenges. Had the circumstances of his life played differently he might've become someone famous, a household name to us all. In fact, I used to shake my head, wondering how notoriety managed to pass him over.

But I don't shake my head anymore. Because over time I learned that our human community is filled with people like him. Many people of no particular status or renown have met their personal challenges with courage and honesty, and then went beyond themselves to help others do the same. Against the odds they have met the challenge to be fully human by being fully alive to, and for, others.

Cast your eye about. I'm going to wager that there is someone near who has quietly made your life better, without fanfare, statues, or brilliant lights. They live just down the street. They walk on the same sidewalk and eat at the same café. They live in an average home and wear average clothing. But they are more than average, because they *do* goodness. They do it in ways that are quiet and unpretentious, not out of false humility, but because they are too busy and too happy being fully human to be concerned for distinction.

As we celebrate the abundance of Nature's food for us, let us also celebrate the abundance of human kindness.

The Turning

The first person I ever heard use the words "shoulder season" was my travel agent. Not summer, when prices and traffic and tempers run high. And not winter, when going anywhere means packing the mukluks or going somewhere warm which, in turn, means going somewhere far. Ah but shoulder, so sweet! The weather is still good, the rates have dropped, and the hordes have returned home. Travel is how I first fell in love with shoulder season. Well, specifically, my thin wallet loved it. But now I have many more reasons. I love it for the near perfection of the light and the air. That a day is warm or a day is cool, but it is neither hot nor cold. That clouds form pictures in the sky, and that greens become yellows, reds and browns. That a day may be dry but it is not searing; that a day may be damp but it is not soggy. I even love that the food in the fields is not as plenteousness, but it is also not altogether scarce. Most of all I love that the light seems sharper, more like "high definition," and that the air has the scent of change to it.

And we are like the autumn. We sense delight for the glistening sun, and we sense melancholy for the same sun's waning. We feel satisfaction for the still abundant Earth, but we are mindful that the dying has begun. There is lassitude at midday, and exigency at day's end. Still so much to do, before it cannot be done: clean and store, mulch the beds, seal the cracks, fasten, stack, gather, cover. Autumn is a miscellany of messages. A jumble of necessities and impending consummations. A mélange of exultations and sorrows. A sense of near-to-completion mingles with the impulse to prepare.

The turning is the shoulder, and portends the cold and the dark. When the chill shrinks everything, and when death treads over life. "*Tetelestai*" said Christ, foretelling all. It is finished.

Yet not. For, puzzling as it may seem, the trajectory of time is at once linear and yet recurring, straight as an arrow, yet spiralling upward. Hence after the waning, and after the dying, there is equal certainty of the rising. The rising will surely come, but after the dying. On a farm, and in every single life, the turning is the time when we celebrate completions, revel in fulfilment, and prepare for the cold that comes closer with every evening dew.

Not So Blind Faith

My father was a salesman, and a good one. No Willy Loman he. He had charm, laughed easily, and walked like an ambassador. He had stories too, one for every occasion. How he grew up poor, how he set out as a young waif and returned to buy up the neighborhood, how his ship got torpedoed, how he went gaga for Mom the first time they ever met. Confident and motivated, Dad did his cold calls without fear. Where others failed to even get a "hello," Dad got in the door and, once inside, found the soft spot. At a factory worker's house he'd quaff a beer and be "just one of the fellas." At a spinster's house he'd sip coffee and cluck sympathetically at snapshots of Bangles, the dearly departed poodle. "Selling is as simple as making the customer your friend," he used to say to me, and I believed him. My father had a lot of insights like that, imperfect pearls cultivated in his own oyster of life. And though he didn't have the genes of an optimist he willed himself to become one, constantly reinforcing himself—and anyone else within earshot— with his home brew of frothy maxims. Dad was a real Norman Vincent Peale type. Made in America. Not a quitter. And, as you might expect, a very talented bullshitter.

Can do. Motivational tapes. Positive vibes. The most stocked books at Chapters. We've heard and seen our culture toss it around since our grandparents were farmers. "Look on the sunny side." But I have an observation to make: my imperfect father and my frivolous culture are largely right. Our mindset matters. Our outlook will determine which way we are moving, in thinking and in life. Humans just seem to do better when they contemplate solutions over problems, bounty over lack, keys over locks. Attitude can flat out change outcomes.

There is, of course, a challenge of some magnitude here, for optimism that fails to acknowledge the hard truths around us is naïve and sometimes dangerous. We must therefore learn that tricky dance between "eyes open" and "nevertheless," words that often step on each other's toes. Still, dance we must, because our personal future, our community, and our planet all want it to be that way. To move from doubt to belief, from pessimism to hope.

Bust Out

Now that the goslings have matured enough to fend for themselves against canines and such, we are free ranging the flock again on the farm. Of course, they were never deprived by spending a good part of the season in their spacious enclosure beside Eleós pond. But try telling that to a goose. As I watched them singlemindedly gorge on the rich cellulose across our land, I could almost hear their goose rejoinder: "Isn't the grass always greener on the other side of the wire?"

In fact, with certain qualifications, it sometimes is. The grass beside the pond may be good enough. But is 'good enough' all that we can hope for? There are times in life when busting out of the boundaries (house, job, debt, lousy relationship, poor habit) is just exactly what we need. To become alive again, to move forward on our path of discovery, and, not least, to contribute more fully to the wealth of human creativity and enrichment. We of the so called 'higher species' learned long ago to temper the visceral urges of instinct, including the very creaturelike urge to 'free range'. On the whole, that's a good thing, too. But who's to say that it's not just as healthy to bust out, when ethical, timely, and expansive busting out is just what we need?

Moving from geese to dogs (I know, it's a lumpy transition), when I returned from the city a few days ago I was met by a mutt in ecstasy. The aforementioned unwieldy Bodie, the rescue dog who came to us three years ago enervated and indifferent to his own canine instincts, came charging in happiness. Bodie the Jubilant! Bodie the Samurai! The once lame dog now doing Fosbury Flops, his clownish, ungainly jetting around making the scene utterly joyous. Bodie of Bust Out Incarnate.

And that's all I mean, really. Geese. Dogs. People. Me. You. Think it through. Or, heck, don't think it through. Let us take our ungainly selves and bust out to our new joy.

Requiem for the Industrial (hu)Man

I step on the remains of a tin can. It dissolves under my foot. My eye sweeps the empty landscape. This is what remains of Garlock, another ore town faded, another onetime boom. I have a fascination for such places, and have journeyed to many of them. Cerro Gordo, Panamint City, Tonopah, New Denver, Randsburg, Ballarat, and many others. I go to them as a pilgrim might go to the sepulchre of a saint. For here is something-that-once-was, and here is pondering. Before me I see the levelling power of the Earth, but with a power that does not brandish. A roof sags but a quarter-inch in a year, and paint bleaches a half-shade in a decade. Imperceptibly, the buildings disintegrate into a jumble of weathered boards. Fly wheels and steam donkeys are frozen like forgotten idols. Ore chutes, stamp mills, smelter chimneys; they all fall prostrate in time. Once there was music here also, once strident horns. Barking dogs. Ecstatic bedsprings. Mournful floorboards. Bubbling pots. Now there is only the flutter of sagebrush.

Like a Creation story told in reverse, the edifices of humankind regress: returning from complexity to primal origins, from dominance to reckoning. This is the end of our doings. This is what we have to show. A weathered brick, a rusted nail, a shard of glass in the sand.

Of course, one need not travel far to see the traces of human makings. From buried cities to microplastic grains on beaches across the globe, the traces are now everywhere. Here at home in the Elphinstone forest I often pass by rotted old cars. Cars that once zoomed along with the radio blasting and a girl and a guy on a bench seat. Now in the space where the windshield once was, a maple sapling grows. On our own land I regularly unearth broken pottery or a piece of forged iron. I examine these small finds, and sometimes put them on the front porch. "Material culture," my son the archeologist calls these. I call them ephemerae, mementos of our impermanence. I say that human cunning is everywhere; and its evanescence everywhere with it. What is this new project of mine? What is the progress to which I contribute?

I am humbled. Earth humbles me. Earth calls for my reverent quiet. But if chastened, I also rejoice. I rejoice that the Earth wields an inexorable, self-healing power. I rejoice that because of it, I cannot be charmed with notions of infinity, nor of eternity, but can only embrace the beauty in, and the gift that is, this very moment.

Yes, just this moment. For truly, there is no other.

Both Sides Now

Call it serendipity. Or kismet. Or fortune. Or Providence. Or possibly just call it the 'the luck of the Irish' (though we are not). This week has been marked by a string of happy surprises. On Monday, Delvin arrived with a tech friend who, unplanned and at no cost, sent his very impressive drone all around and high above the farm, taking high resolution images that we will be able to use to know more exactly this land, and therefore to know better how to steward it. On Tuesday, friends Rick and Carole overnighted, bringing with them Jay and Sharon, a botanist and an ethnobotanist respectively. We walked the property to identify various hitherto mysterious trees, shrubs and plants. What a gift! On Wednesday Val completed and released a fine video of the Brookbank Farm enterprise, of food issues, and of the fine community that joins together to be the change they want to see. That's not a bad start to the week, don't you think?

Gaia, God, Luck, the Universe, positive mindedness. Call it whatever you like, but there's a deeper power at work. Sometimes we just get happily surprised by people and events working in our favour. When we feel the weight of life's challenges and inequities, we do well to remember also that kindnesses, generosity, small mercies and large graces, are equally everywhere. Whether subtle or bold, plainspoken or secret, *they are everywhere*. The Universe will so conspire.

4D

A few nights ago Dawn and I curled up on the sofa and went surfing for a movie. What is the mood tonight? Do we go with "heartwarming romantic comedy" or "period piece"? "edge-of-your-seat thriller!" or "cinematic masterpiece"? Ah decisions. Admittedly, from time to time we are still seduced by the trailers, and by public opinion as expressed on iMDB and such. "Oh honey, this one gets a 7.3 rating! Let's give it a try!" 7.3 is right up there, so we do. It's a sci-fi attempt, of course another digital eye popper, of course all far gone apocalyptic, and of course—when it had to go Matrix on us—another uninspiring effort. You know the feeling: Been there, done that.

Or is it us? People were once spellbound when silents became talkies. Until they weren't. Ditto black and white to colour. Same again those 3D monster shows of the fifties, and lately reborn in Avatar. Star Wars reignited our captivation for space/time travel, but today we yawn through another one. Disaster films? Zzzzz. High speed chase? b-o-r-i-n-g. Pyrotechnics? Unremitting bloodshed? Heroic victories? What does it take to keep our attention today, to make us feel delighted, filled, stirred, inspired? While the film business churns out another blockbuster lookalike, we have already strayed.

Far be it from me to pooh pooh the exhilaration we humans crave. Adventure, newness, pushing the edges of our imagination, enlarging our world (inner and outer), all good. But thrills often come cheap, and like anything cheap, they don't last.

There is another kind of exhilaration, however. It is not incumbent upon being momentarily wowed, horrified, or scared out of your gourd. It derives instead from something or somewhere deeper, equally refreshing, but differently so. I'm not sure it can even be captured in words. It happened to me this week as I cast an eye about the farm and there saw our farmers and helpers variously pruning, harvesting, hoeing, and weeding. We were working together. We had worthy purposes. The sun, the season, the soil, the ripening food, the sweat, the talk, the intuitive richness of participating rather than being entertained. Everything coalesced for me to become, well, thrilling. Do you get my meaning, friends?

When 4D glasses are invented, I'll line up with you at the theatre. We'll love it. But while being so wowed, let's remember the things that *actually thrill us* (and not merely titillates our senses). What stirs you? Inspires you? You will know what they are when they take your breath away the morning after, and after that, and after that. These are what matter. Chase those thrills. Because these are the beacons for your life.

Humanity on the Rise

Lately I have been wondering again what it will all come to. Politics has finally morphed into pure entertainment, but alas, less of the Disney variety and more of the Rocky Horror kind. Xenophobia is on the rise again. Africa disintegrates with Bokom Haram and a hundred other militia-terrorist armies. The Philippines. Thailand. Afghanistan. Palestine. Columbia. The UN currently lists more than five dozen countries where there is armed conflict. That's a lot of fear, and a lot of loathing. There are pandemics and pestilences aplenty. Food is becoming scarcer as our soils erode and our oceans become giant trash bins. With the trees falling and the engines of humans burning, the carbon is getting ahead of us, and the world is getting hotter. These 'big picture' realities, they are difficult to grasp, much less to do something about. I wonder, why do wars seem to remain a legitimate option for resolving differences? Why do those who have the most still want more? Why do we not care better for our planetary home, the only home we have? My questions do not have easy answers. Sometimes I want to hide from it all. But then I know that my community is the whole community, the whole world. I am also something of a longer for deliverance, if you will; the mystic-hoper who believes that to send our aid near and far, our concern, our prayers, our conversation, our unspoken, formidable *hopefulness,* is not futile.

Circumspection is always advised. For the bleak side of life is but one side of life. One of our food buyers has gifted her purchase to a family in need. A single kindness such as this—no spectacle, no heroism—has more weight than a cannon. In time, and when kindnesses such as these multiply one upon another, the cannon itself will finally be rendered futile. Do you share this belief with me? that every small goodness we do is a world-altering event?

This is our human story, of course. Two steps forward and one back. To go forward without any expectation of regression along the way is not being realistic. Thankfully, the guardians of evolution and increased human knowledge prevent us from freefalling completely; that step back is but one step. Step by step we go, and along that journey we will witness the slow death of war, the demise of prejudice, and the end of want. Dying is not serene, but it is certain. The people out willing the unwilling, loving their neighbour, and respecting the planet will make certain that with time, and with loving choices, we will overcome. I am remembering this today: Two steps forward, but only one back.

When Thanatos Crashes the Party

I was a boy when Neil Armstrong aimed his camera lens across the Bay of Tranquility to capture an image of our planetary home that gobsmacked the world. Beyond the foreground of a stark lunar landscape, enveloped in a black darkness everywhere, the Earth shimmers like a blue sapphire swirled with milky clouds. We knew it all along, but seeing it like that made us gasp. It is beautiful, it is alive, it is perfect. On Venus our shoes would melt even if they were made of lead. On Jupiter we'd have to say "Honey, I'm going out on a walk to get some fresh ammonia." On Neptune we'd only blow out birthday candles once every 164 years. But Earth, our spaceship home, is ideally located, and contains the ideal cocktail of elements, for Life to proliferate. Kaboom! From the tiniest protozoa to the great blue whale, millions of species flourish here. Imagine: a single handful of soil may contain more living organisms than there are people on Earth! We are everywhere, flying, crawling, swimming, wriggling, running, walking, and merely sitting our way into the continuance of our own. Earth is a grand festival, a jubilee of dance, food, sex and more sex.

But nothing lives long. One species may live for mere seconds, another for a century, but in the vast wheel of time both are nothing. Because we are just that, *animated*, hardwired to crave life and to go on living, we often neglect to ponder the fact that everything living will also cease to live. But in this very second, whatever astronomically high number represents life on Earth, death is equal to it. It's a perfect equation. Death and Life are competing in an endless tie.

Not only do we not naturally dwell on this fact, when we set out to do so, we haven't much help. For life can be observed, seen under a microscope, charted, categorised, and now even modified. But death? It merely Is. It is the blackness around the sapphire. As life-cravers, we avoid it. As scientists, we scratch our heads. As religionists, we can only manage to ease the angst of it. And when death happens, most of us get the "oh no" feeling. A sadness, a melancholy. A moment of quiet, when the subconscious does its rigorous check in: nothing lives long. This morning I went out to feed the hens. We lost one. The death of a chicken is not something I grieve deeply. But here was a hen that gave us eggs, ate pests, and made more than a few children smile. Huddled in a corner of the coop, she sat still in her death, frozen in place like a lunar landscape. I thanked Providence for her, and buried her beside a blueberry bush. She is food now for the Earth, and part of the dance of Life and of Death, in the dance that will never end.

One Person To Hear You

Circumstances have me thinking today of a few special people, and thinking further that it is good to be thankful for them just now. Tommy, my 'first' best friend, a carrot top kid who always turned crimson under the California sun. I remember that we circled wide at first, for I questioned that a red head could be trusted, and he thought it freakish that I had a lookalike twin brother. But we overcame these hesitancies. In winter we rode together on the Bluebird bus, seated in the very back where the driver couldn't survey us. In summer we ran barefoot, dodging spike thorns and red ants, daring one another to cross the oven hot asphalt street. We watched in awe and sadness together the day our 'wilderness', the orange grove across the street, got pushed over by bulldozers.

Then the fateful day happened. Tommy told me he would be moving. "To a place called 'Escondido'" he announced, which sounded, and effectively was, like moving to the Moon. Our friendship had come to a perilous time. And so instinctively (for what else could it have been?) we went to the wilderness of an orchard still standing, and there selected a sharp thistle. We pushed our thumbs into the thorn, and when tiny drops of red emerged we rubbed our thumbs together, and swore our fealty: blood brothers forever. We were eight years old, Tommy did move, and I have never seen him since.

The human hunger for friendship begins early and never ends. Each of us has one at least, a special 'someone' who we might say is our 'best friend.' Who is yours? Someone who not only answers the inexplicable inner spiritual longing for another, but supports us to become all we are meant to be? Creative. Safe. Heard. Held. Happy. While many commentators muse on the profundities of romantic or divine love, I give my nod just now to the power and the beauty of *phileo*. Said Ovid long ago, "Love is born in friendship's name."

Dream On

If you are a product of old time Sunday School, and have good recall, you might remember the story of Joseph, the youngest of Jacob's twelve sons. Skipping the details and getting right to the grist, Joseph suffered the spite of his smallminded siblings, and in consequence, endured several Ancient Near Eastern raw deals. Picked on. Shunned. Tossed into a pit. Sold into slavery. Et Cetera. You see, Joseph was odd, and being odd, he was misunderstood. He was also smarter by half than his Luddite brothers, but that's not really what annoyed them. The real threat to them was that their younger brother was a dreamer. Not just idyllic reveries. I mean crazy, Technicolor dreams. Dreams of the future. Dreams of what is possible. As the story progresses, despite all the repudiation, hardships, long stints in Third World jails and such, Joseph never stopped dreaming. The ending to the story is all Hollywood: eventually those dreams would rescue him. Raise him up. Make him great. His dreams even saved a whole nation from ruin. Joseph becomes a national hero for it, clothed in finery, drinking tea with the nobles. As a moral postscript, when his contemptible brothers turn up starved and bedraggled, though nobody would have blinked if Joseph had them all sent to the gallows, he forgives the whole lot of them.

This week a friend of mine asked me "where I want to be." Translated, he was asking me to be a dreamer again. At first I was nonplussed. Skipping this or that farm project I need to complete, or grant to write (which I do for a nonprofit organization), or even certain year end goals I have set, I haven't truly *dreamed* in a while. I haven't tapped into the crazy, into the Technicolour, into what is possible or possibly what is impossible but who cares if it is or it isn't? Instead I had let myself somewhat mechanically tramp along through middle age, and thinking myself too old to dream now.

My friend gave me a healthy jolt out of my walking somnolence. Of course it's time to get Technicolor again, because it always is! Against any 'best-be-careful' reticence, paper tigers of fear, faux-wisdom-with-age it's *always time* to get hungry again for possibilities, personal and far beyond. To imagine a future where there are no barriers to what we might become. Best of all, we can dream large. That's right: No dream is too crazy, or too improbable, because whether they materialize or not is, in fact, secondary. More importantly, more vitally, it is dreams that get us up in the morning. It is dreams that set our visionary eye to a fair horizon. Therefore dreams are the world changers. The people changers. The 'me' changers, and the 'you' changers too.

I Read the News Today Oh Boy

This morning the newspaper came wrapped inside a political ad. The ad told me that the promises of the opponent cannot be kept without bankrupting me. It told me that if I vote instead for the good guy I am certain to enjoy greater personal affluence, and the peace of knowing there's not a bomb under the local bus. And other such possibilities. I took a swig of stiff coffee, and peeled off that ad with all the reverence of peeling dead skin off my heel. Alas, in the dermis beneath I fared little better, the banner story lauding the merits of nuclear energy. I drained my coffee.

It's so easy to get down, isn't it? When the autumnal equinox is weeks gone, and the hemisphere prepares to quiet itself in cold. When the news is the news is the news. And, yes, when the ocean of empty promises that is politics rises faster even than the waters of our warming planet.

I am presently coffeed and now determined, however, to put the black dog out of my house. I am deciding instead, right here and now, to make some promises of my own.

I promise to embrace this most normal and natural "season of melancholy" and yet temper it with memories of how spectacular are my friends and family, the food I eat, and the good land upon which I dwell.

I promise to be alive to the struggle of our times and the news that often hurts; but I will also keep a visionary eye to the horizon of hope and change.

I promise to vote. I will not vote because one or another party is better at promise making. Really, who is that naïve? I will vote instead to help fulfil my own promises. I promise to love and respect the Earth, to honour my community and its people, to live by the ethic of fairness, and to err on the side of peace. Most of all, I promise to wrest that hackneyed and promise-killing adjective "solemn" from my promises, instead grasping my promises as I might a bouncing beach ball, bouncing across the room of my soul, colourful, playful, joyful. Nothing but joyful.

I'd Like To Do Something Good for Matilde

Roberto and I stood under a piece of tin in the village of Zapote, waiting out another downpour. We shared that shelter with a *campesina* and her boy of perhaps ten. The boy was wearing a T-shirt with a silk screened message across the front that read, "Celtics Soccer Club, Warren County Ohio." I venture he did not get that shirt in Ohio. In Honduras incongruous messages are everywhere on the backs of the poor. In Minas de Oro I saw, "Vietnam Vets Outreach, Erie, Pennsylvania," and in Mal Paso, "Gainsville Chapter of the American Legion." Alejandra's T shirt announced that "Somebody loves me in Idaho." And then there is Matilde and his shirt. Matilde is a slight man with a mischievous eye and a giant heart. A man of optimism and the fire of life in his eyes. He has so little to his name, but that does not stop him from saying that he is blessed. "Dios y la vida son buenos," he says. Matilde is the kind of person you are always glad to be around. When I met Matilde he was wearing a shirt that featured a cartoon of a drunk and the words "35% Alcohol by Volume." How could I tell him that his shirt was probably a frat boy's cast off, and who had more beer money for a week than Matilde had for food in a month?

Shirts leave our shores sold as rags. In great, compressed bundles, thousands of tons are shipped abroad. But once those bundles arrive, they are gleaned, and rags are sold again as clothing. The detritus of a rich land is flat out salvaged by another. This thought gives me pause. There is so much I might consider. I want to reflect on our place in the world community. I want to find new ways to join with people near and far in life-affirming ways. I want to learn from Matilde about resourcefulness, and the appreciation of things small. I want to find peaceful ways of repudiating consumptive economies and the giant, faceless businesses that put profit before people. I want to share with others my belief that there is a direct link between purchasing local food and goods, and cast off T-shirts in Honduras. And while economics and politics drive the world to inequitable ends, I want right here, right now, to do something good for Matilde. For all change of any value always only begins small, and always only with me and with you.

In The Not So Bleak Midwinter

Winter only officially begins with the Solstice on or about the 21st of December. But calendar designations-of-humans are sometimes laughable. For Nature—she of supreme power and she of coquettish fun—has just jumped behind the wheel of an Arctic sedan for a crazy, fishtailing ride. Whee! she lets out, as she crosses the wheels again.

Meanwhile we sit in the back seat with clenched teeth, at once terrified and thrilled. But give it a minute, and the terror weakens. This is all fun. What was recently the schlop schlop across Brookbank Farm 'wetlands' is now the crunch of a sparkling carpet underfoot. I stoop down to see it closer. Such an infinity of crystalline patterns! And the squadrons of dragonflies that danced in summer over the surface of Eliós pond have metamorphosed into snowflakes, gamboling this way and that across the frozen water. New heralds of the world as undulations! But silent heralds, for there is no sound but the pillowy quiet that only snow can accomplish. And the thrill in me strengthens.

Suddenly, like a gift, the Mysteries—those invisible powers of earth, wind, fire, breath, and providence—momentarily lift their veils to reveal near smiles, like the Mona Lisa. Demure, knowing smiles. I smile right back, grateful for this sudden glimpse. Grateful also that I dismissed the soulish whimper of the ex-pat Californian within me and instead climbed into my thermals, plunked a toque on my head, and went out to the land.

I take it all in, just now, for the severe beauty of it, and for the soul's banquet there. For when will I next walk this farm with nothing to plant, to weed, to harvest, to build, with nothing at all to do but to relish its nothing-to-do-ness? And when will I next see a mystery, and see my breath float dreamily away?

Your New Hat Looks Fabulous

Résumés: Dawn has a degree in geography and once worked in IT. I have my gilded certificates in theology and once worked in the ministry. In and between those pasts we have both worked a variety of gigs-for-pay. Today we farm. And by the way, I never did become an archeologist. That's right. Long before Indiana Jones had everyone running out to buy a sable fedora, I decided that when I grew up that's what I would be. Spawned by my father's vast collection of National Geographic magazines, and being the prototypical kid, I dreamt of discovering treasures and lost cities. Another Troy. Another Rosetta Stone. Another Xanadu.

In high school the question "What are you going to be?" fell like a millstone out of the sky. After all, it was time to begin Life-As-An-Adult. You were expected to know by then, so much so that the naming of your future occupation was inscribed, more like an epitaph than a prognostication, beneath your grad photo in the school Annual. That most of us did not really know what we wanted to be should've made us question the value of 'vocational profiling' even then. Didn't we much prefer the immediacy of a baseball game, or watching girls at the Newport pier? Didn't we dream about *adventuring* more than accountancy, nursing, or soldiering?

The social anthropologists say that vocational choices are the product of the Industrial Age. Before then you were what your father (or mother) was. But I think we should give Nature some credit too. Skipping for a moment all the changes Dawn and I have imposed on the landscape at Brookbank Farm, I need only look to the untouchable area on our farm, the "wild zone" on the southern edge. The lesson of Nature there is plain faced. The swimming hole at the creek we enjoyed when we first arrived is almost gone. Some trees have grown spectacularly. Others not. A huge maple tree has fallen, and a fir—where is it?—has literally vanished. All this and much more in just four years since we began observing it. What I mean is that Nature (of which we are a part) is not stuck into one anything. Never has been either! Nature is ever and always adventuring, changing its strategy, morphing its landscape, searching for greater abundance, courting fecundity, greening and beautifying, moving, wandering, and ever reaching for the sun. In the core of each of us, on the seat of our soul, sits no vocation. If there is something you have always wanted to do, now is the time to do it. It is never too late to begin a new adventure, a new vocation, a new anything. While we have life and breath, it is never not time to discover new landscapes and greater abundance, ever reaching for the sun. Me? I think I may go get that sable fedora yet.

Elphinstone in the Mist

It is the month of ghostly fruit trees
and of the fallen bird.
When the circle closes
to keep within an ember,
and there see the need to be reborn.

The creek is keening in lament
to an unknown ending.
And light is but a tendril
that will cast no shadow,
but merely show a breath drift away.

The tools hang on pegs as if crucified,
the tractor seat is tilted forward.
All things in obeisance
to the silent power.
We also, bowed in veneration.

A drop of mist is a gemstone
that holds the whole world,
But strange to me, strangely so,
for the whole world is upside down.

Now the wood stove hums its cradlesong,
where boots are set to dry.
Here there are thoughts, reminders
of what will be again.
Here is where dreams are devotion.

Great land, great sky and mountain above,
Small creature I, below.
We live by your beckoning,
embers to become flames.
When you will call for the abundance again.

It is the month of waiting.
Elphinstone is silent in the mist.
We are that circle waiting
to be born, and after,
to be reborn.

Coda

It is a day of damp to the bones chilliness, the rain presently a vertical ocean, and the filmy gray light of morning acting pretender to sunshine. Even if it were clear today, the sky would only lighten well after the morning coffee now. We go to work in the dark and come home in the dark. We stack the firewood by the porch for easy reach. We drape the Adirondack chairs in plastic, lay up the garden tools, and think about possibly going away to some place where the bones will get warm again.

All of which is perfectly apropos to the moment, when we say around the room to one another "thank you". We are grateful for those who purchase our farm goods, and far beyond the "commerce" of it, for what it means: eating for better health, supporting local economies, loving the planet, and building a community. We know that it is sometimes easier to wheel a steel cart past 40,000 choices (the average number of items stocked in a supermarket). We know that it is sometimes cheaper (but not in the big picture) to go to the "big box" store. We know that the odd blemish on the locally grown food is a thing to get used to. We know that you know that farming is a circus act with an uncertain outcome: weather, experimentation, and the whims of economies being just a few of the volatile factors. We are therefore doubly grateful for you. We are also grateful for this good land with its excellent soil, abundant water, and many trees. For this land that nourishes us and you. For this land that speaks wisdom into our hearts, and carries us into the new day.

New Mercies

As sunrises go, I've seen better. The sky went modestly from amber to pale blue. But sometimes context is everything, because this sunrise proved to be one of my most memorable. I was on Temple IV in the ruins of Tikal, the once great capital of a vast and powerful Mayan civilization. To climb Temple IV, I had to slip under a fence with a warning sign on it not to do such a thing. The infraction, and the consequent risk of the steep climb itself, only heightened my anticipation. When I got to the summit I discovered that my idea was in fact not so novel; several others were already there. But we did not profane the event with "hellos" and "good mornings." Instead, scattered as we were atop this magnificent work of human ingenuity and power, each of us held our own personal silence. Whatever God we worshipped then, whatever thoughts passed through our minds, they were sacred to us alone. I had mine, and while they remain cached in my soul, I will share one thought here.

I reflected on how I was standing in an unbroken succession of humankind who for millennia has shared an intrinsic, indomitable, and relentless longing: we long for the new day. The sunrise, the sun god, the temple built to that god, the advent of a new beginning, the genesis of new opportunities, the rebirth of a hope busting through a rock, a snowbank, a life change, a once interminable darkness. A renaissance, a recharge, a renewal, a resurrection.

Soon now the soil will begin to warm, and with it our hopefulness. The season of food, friendship and connection to one another once again lightens our archetypal sky overhead. It is the dawn. I welcome the coming of the day with all its wondrous possibilities. For mercies come new every morning, of this I am now sure.

One

One dream one hope
When a day is a thousand years
and a thousand years a day

One joy one desire
When the circle that is life
is to live now and to live well

One fullness one completion
When the stream that is abundance
pours over its banks

One dream one hope
When our children's children
say that we became all that we were meant to be

Acknowledgements

Special thanks are given to my partner Dawn for her candid feedback, proofreading, and near perfect patience in this project and in the project of life together; and to Delvin Solkinson, friend and permaculture master teacher, who leapt into the graphic work with his trademark enthusiasm and skill.

The title of this work is inspired by the late Paul Tillich, who opposed the traditional language of theism, calling instead for us to imagine God as the "ground of being." His efforts to find a new language for a new time opened dialogue between those who contemplate deeper meanings, but differently so.

This collection is dedicated to the many people who support locally grown, healthy food marketed through the Gibsons Farm Collective, and to those visionaries everywhere who share the dream of a better future.

Photo Credits

All photos taken at Brookbank Farm with the exception of Unveilings (Elphinstone forest), The Unseen Real (Elphinstone forest), One Person To Hear You (Anaheim, Ca.), and I'd Like To do Something Good For Matilde (Minas de Oro, Honduras).

Deep gratitude to the following contributors:

Aaron Cambrin
Sui Generis; We of the Larger Brain; Make It Beautiful; The Angel Next Door.

Adrian Myers
The Low Hanging Fruit.

Charlie Durrant
What a Dreamer, They Say; Surrounding Myself With You; DIY; Requiem for the Industrial (hu)Man; 4D; Montage #1; Montage #7; author photo.

Ryan Hill
Montage #1.

Dawn Myers
Do the Hokey Pokey; Counterpower; Unveilings; Predict-Me-Not; Carpe Momentum; Living On the Edges; The Ground of Our Being; Scratching the Surface; To Do; Nice Package is No Package; Sector Surrender; A Wallet Awakening; What Makes It Tick; Not So Blind Faith; Bust Out; Your New Hat Looks Fabulous; One; Montage #2; Montage #3, Montage #6.

Paul Myers
Introduction; My Dirty Old Man; The Blessed Mess; E Aye E Aye O; Defeating the Defeatist Within; Living In the Time Between; Mementos for Amnesiacs; Predict-Me-Not, the Sequel; A Summer Salad Like a Rapture; De and Re Generation, Bo Bo Be aBarkin'; The Be-Attitudes; C'Mon Then, Clouds. You Can Do It; K.I.S.S. (Keep It Simple Sage); The Unseen Real; Corny Ain't So Bad; The Turning; Both Sides Now; When Thanatos Crashes the Party; Dream On; I Read the News Today Oh Boy; I'd Like to Do Something Nice for Matilde; In the Not So Bleak Midwinter; Elphinstone In the Midst; Coda; New Mercies; Montage #5.

Sunshine Coast Museum and Archives
Make Hay; Humanity on the Rise.

Dana Wilson
Less Work, Thank You: The (under)Graduate; Montage #4.

About the Author

Paul Myers has walked a rich and varied journey of life, and has no intention of letting it get boring now. He is widely travelled, has lived in five countries, and along the way completed three postgraduate degrees (MCS, MDiv, DTh). Ordained in 1993, Paul served as minister in Vancouver and West Vancouver, BC. He moved to Gibsons, BC in 2006, taking with him the conviction that people and the planet matter, that spiritual sweat of any kind is still the best kind, and that the nonviolent power of few can sway many. In 2008 he and his spouse Dawn began Backyard Bounty, a spin farming business, which later became Brookbank Farm. With others, they also founded the Gibsons Farm Collective. Paul has completed the Permaculture Design Course and the advanced Diploma in Permaculture Design. He also works for a nonprofit with at-risk youth in Vancouver. Paul is the author of two books and several award-winning short stories.